Contemporary Christologies:
A Jewish Response

Eugene B. Borowitz

PAULIST PRESS
New York/Ramsey

Copyright © 1980 by
Eugene B. Borowitz

Library of Congress
Catalog Card Number: 80-81051

ISBN: 0-8091-2305-3

Published by Paulist Press
Editorial Office: 1865 Broadway, New York, N.Y. 10023
Business Office: 545 Island Road, Ramsey, N.J. 07446

Printed and bound in the
United States of America

Contents

to
Nathaniel and Marjorie Hess

I. Introduction: On the Context of a Challenge

Nothing so divides Judaism and Christianity as the Christian doctrine of the Christ. If Jews and Christians are to talk together for more than pragmatic reasons, they must confront this area of their radical disagreement. In medieval times, Jews, Christians and Moslems agreed on the standards of proper intellectuality and could confront one another's doctrine at considerable depth. Today we have lost the medieval confidence in objective reason and, instead, appreciate the meta-rational nature of faith. The existentialists seem to have made their point that belief is grounded in so elemental a level of the self that it cannot adequately be rendered in propositional form.

That would seem to rule out any meaningful theological confrontation between faiths. Indeed, this is the classic modern Orthodox Jewish explanation of the refusal to enter intertheological discussions (Soloveitchik, 1964*). Even if one does not propose to adopt the existentialist stance, pressing the personal side of belief to such lengths, it seems clear that no universal basis for interreligious debate is easily available. It should not be surprising then that little philosophic attention has been paid to the logic of interreligious discourse, William A. Christian's *Oppositions of Religious Doctrines* excepted.

Indeed, what is asserted most fervently by a given faith gen-

---

* For ease of reproduction, notes are given in the text only by author, date of publication and page (in the case of direct quotation). The bibliography provides full data. Where a citation is continuous only the page number is given.

1

erally produces the most bitter debate among its own adherents.
For Christians that has certainly been true of the doctrine of the
Christ (by comparison, for Jews it applies to the meaning and
entailments of Torah). Such disagreement may be of a minor
nature, the disputants recognizing that what divides them is relatively insignificant. Should the issues become more troublesome, dissent may nonetheless be accepted because it is viewed
dialectically. That is, the differing views are seen as part of a
greater unity the believers share (today's ecumenicism).

Already at this stage the logical problems begin to mount,
for the limits to heterodox belief are usually unarticulated. Intrareligious debate may become sufficiently intense so that
those involved wonder whether they and their antagonists continue to share the same faith. Outsiders, not being privy to the
importance of the issue involved, may remain impressed by the
common belief that still distinguishes the disputants from other
religionists. At the same time, those in the debate may sense
having approached or crossed a religious boundary. This often
engenders a logically odd form of religious statement, of which
some assertions by Jurgen Moltmann are a good example. He
writes, "All Christian statements about God, about creation,
about sin and death have their focal point in . . ." or "Christianity cannot therefore any longer be represented as . . ." or
"Christian faith is not . . ." (1974, pp. 204, 215).

Moltmann and others who make such statements know that
many Christians disagree with them and they have no authority
to declare the opposing views meaningless. This does not deter
them from making such dogmatic utterances, a pattern of self-
conscious incoherence worthy of the attention of open-minded
linguistic analysts.

In the extreme, dissent becomes heresy. Then some dissi-
dents are ruled to be standing outside the community of believers. When the permissible limits of belief in this area have not
previously been clarified, the alleged heresy will call forth a
fresh self-definition by the religion. The result may be that certain patterns of belief are declared to be anathema now, though
somehow they were not so previously. What once seemed to be

only dissent and thus tolerable is now seen as inconsistent with proper faith and can no longer be borne.

The logic of intrareligious difference is therefore critical in understanding the theological change that characterizes religion. From this point of view, to limit the study of religious usage to questions of coherence gives too much weight to what has been static in religion. Both continuity and development must be given their due in any effort to analyze the structures of the religious "language game."

If those who once shared a faith can wonder whether they have a common universe of discourse, how much more will this be true of believers who speak from divergent world views. Interreligious discussion therefore creates many more problems for those who would not only wish to share their beliefs but to debate them.

My philosophical curiosity was therefore immediately aroused by the invitation of the American Theological Society to provide one of the two papers on contemporary christologies for discussion at the 1975 annual meeting. I felt that a detailed investigation of a theological area in which Christianity and Judaism have radically different views would provide many intriguing cases for the logic of interreligious discussion. Working from the specific problems that arose in the various theological confrontations to the general logical considerations involved in such antagonistic discourse proved highly fruitful. But I forbear entering into its results here, allowing the various philosophical issues to emerge below in relation to the doctrinal discussions that engendered them.

There was, obviously, also a substantive reason for undertaking this study. If Jewish-Christian discussions are to prove meaningful, the issues inherent in the Christian doctrine of the Christ must be squarely faced. To the best of my knowledge no Jew in modern times has done this on a theological level, that is, by studying and responding to what contemporary Christian theologians are saying about Jesus as the Christ. To a considerable extent, a similar comment may be made about the medieval disputations between the faiths. Those debates commonly centered on the exegetical issue of whether Jesus of Nazareth had fulfilled the Jewish expectations of the coming of the Messiah. They almost never touched on Christian theological descriptions of the nature and the work of Jesus as the Christ (Talmage, 1975, pp. 56ff). One of the surprises of this study was the extent to which argument from biblical texts was peripheral rather than central to contemporary christology, including the presentations of the traditionalists among the theologians to whom I was directed. (In this regard, see particularly Chapter III below.) Jews today may still find their old exegetical arguments useful against those missionaries who persist in trying to prove that Jesus fulfilled the biblical prophecies concerning the Messiah. They will not thereby have engaged, much less made their case against, sophisticated contemporary doctrines of the Christ.

The most common Jewish approach to Christianity these days is historical. In part that stems from the loss of confidence in revelation which was a major by-product of the emancipation and modernization of European Jewry in the nineteenth century. In larger part, it represents a strategic choice of ground that yields the Jewish debater an initial advantage in the discussion of Christian claims for Jesus. When this topic is treated in a strictly historical fashion, the positivism implicit in most versions of the proper academic treatment of ancient sources places an almost impossible burden of proof on the protagonists of Jesus' Christ-hood. The historical approach has another advantage from the Jewish point of view. It allows the Jewish historians to reject the major assertion of Christian faith without ever having to raise the troublesome question of their own beliefs. (For a comprehensive account of Jewish academic scholarship in this area see Sandmel, 1965.)

When modern Jewish thinkers have sought to contrast their faith with that of Christians, their treatments of the other religion seem tendentious and subjective. Instead of facing up to the highly variegated and richly nuanced christologies of their Christian analogues they have preferred to deal with a popular image of the Christ or a figure of their own creation. In either case their consequent rejection of Christian doctrine carries little conviction for it does not deal with the opponent's strongest case. The methodological lessons to be learned from their examples are sufficiently important so that I should like to explore two key instances of Jewish discussions of Christianity that ignored theological treatments of the nature and work of the Christ.

Hermann Cohen and his syncretistic disciple Leo Baeck, both Jewish neo-Kantians, are so determinedly polemical that they can see only the Christianity they wish to refute. Both define Judaism and Christianity in such a way that the former is far more appealing to the modern spirit. For Cohen, Christianity is insufficiently rational. Its God is traditionally trinitarian or, in modern guise, so immanent as to be ethically impotent. Furthermore its ethics are inadequate, for Christianity stresses faith and neglects the Kantian insight that moral obligation must take the form of law. Judaism, by contrast, is essentially an ethical monotheism and thus history's finest exemplar of what reason teaches a religion should be. (See Cohen, 1972, the entry "Christ" in the index of proper names, p. 483.)

Baeck continues Cohen's line of argument, as the structure and content of the second part of *The Essence of Judaism* shows (1961, pp. 83ff†). However, Baeck is not a pure philosophic rationalist but is concerned with religious consciousness (Borowitz, 1961, pp. 79ff). He therefore characterizes the two faiths as representing two types of religiosity, the classical and the romantic, though each shares something of the piety of the other. Christianity is the romantic religion *par excellence*. It is fundamentally emotional, individualistic, and transrational. It stresses faith, creates dependency, and focuses the religious life on sacrament and miracle. Judaism is the great example of a classical religion. It is essentially rational, activist, structured by commandment and the consequent life of intellect, and as much concerned with community as it is with the individual. (The essay "Romantic Religion" is in Baeck, 1958, pp. 189ff.)

Cohen and Baeck argued against the most passive interpretation of Christianity of their time. They would not have had far

---

† Friedlander (1968, pp. 51ff) sees the book as a response to Harnack, but I believe Baeck's debt to Harnack is greater than any alleged polemic against him.

to go to seek Protestant thinkers whoe appreciation for universi-
ty-trained, cultured, politically active burghers was as great as
theirs. Much of Cohen's hermeneutic of Judaism was derived—
creatively, to be sure—from the churchless but Protestant Kant,
while Baeck's approach to Judaism was heavily indebted to the
gentiles Schleiermacher, Otto and Dilthey. Moreover, their interpretations of Judaism—Cohen's "ideal" Judaism; Baeck's
"essence"—were radical reinterpretations of what traditional Judaism understood itself to be. They taught a modernist, German, liberal interpretation of their faith but rejected the idea
that Christianity might have an equal right to a neo-Kantian interpretation. That would have compromised their polemic agenda. Surely their confrontation with Christianity would have been
more significant had they argued with their modernizing Christian equivalents.

Martin Buber, partially in opposition to liberals like Cohen
and Baeck, eschewed philosophic speculation and sought reality
in confrontation with persons. For him, Christianity might best
be understood by openness to the life and teaching of Jesus of
Nazareth. By studying what the New Testament had to say about
him, Buber also hoped to direct himself to what was shared by
all Christians, despite their differing theologies. In his work *Two
Types of Faith,* Buber appears to be making a conscientious effort
to be open to the person testified to in the text, though he admits he is reading it with Jewish eyes. In the Foreword he acknowledges the guidance of Rudolf Bultmann with regard to
methods of New Testament exegesis, and his footnotes show his
reading in other Protestant scholarly works (1951, p. 13). He
thus studies the text with the full range of philological and historical tools, without forgetting what those who believe in the
holiness of the text say it means.

Yet Buber subordinates all this to what his I-Thou hermeneutic reveals to him, a personal Jesus who must radically be distinguished from the Christ of Christianity. Buber thought that
by employing his unique method he would find the truth about
Jesus. To most modern students of the New Testament Buber
seems to have confronted a Jesus figure substantially of his own
devising. Since Buber was so extraordinary a religious spirit his

subjective reading of the text has intrinsic interest. But Buber is not a useful guide if one wishes to come to know the Jesus of contemporary liberal New Testament scholarship or of Christian doctrine.

Perhaps the most important lesson we have learned about interpersonal and interreligious dialogue in recent years is that we must make a determined effort to get to know people as they are, not as we, for whatever reason, would have them be. I do not see, then, that Christians and Jews can come to understand one another better unless they address each other's mature theologies. This can most readily be done in areas where there are common or overlapping beliefs. Yet it will not produce its most significant results until it focuses on the matters wherein they disagree radically with one another. The doctrine of the Christ seems a critical case in point and it was with this in mind that I accepted the American Theological Society's invitation to prepare a paper on contemporary christology.

Since I speak from a standpoint of personal faith that informs my academic concerns, I think it important to be open with my readers and present my personal position within my religious community. From the examples given above it seems clear that until we know the context from which authors speak—skeptical, mystic, liberal, orthodox—we will have difficulty evaluating the judgments they make. Permit me, therefore, to situate myself religiously. I am a Jew whose existence is grounded in the people of Israel's Covenant with God. I am not a *halachic* Jew, which is to say that I am not a Jew who believes that the only authentic way to live in the Covenant is to observe the discipline laid down in the Bible, the Talmud and the classic Jewish codes as interpreted by the Orthodox sages of our generation. I try to live in the piety and discipline of Torah, by which I mean seeking to understand and act on what God wants of me now as a member of this covenanted people and a continuator of its heritage. In terms of the relatively obsolete denominational labels we still use, I am a Reform Jew of religiously traditional bent. I speak from the context of the right wing of liberal Judaism. I suggest that in reacting to contemporary christologies, my views are characteristic of a broad sweep of Jewish opinion. This judg-

ment is subjective but not unfounded. In my broad acquaintance
with Jewish thought and thinkers I find substantial consensus in
our approach to Christianity. While we may disagree on what we
affirm, we are reasonably well united on what we do not believe.
Nonetheless, since I am sensitive to the plurality of opinion in
the Jewish community, I shall indicate, when appropriate, where
our internal Jewish divisions produce differing responses to
Christian claims.

Finally, it seems to me self-evident that to discuss someone
else's faith one should first have a reasonably accurate understanding of it, that is, one that would be recognized and acknowledged as knowledgeable by its informed adherents.
Judaism has often been sinned against in this regard by scholars
who described it as an arid legalism or denied its continuing piety before God, or ignored its religious creativity after the destruction of the Second Temple, or mistook noncanonical books
for normative Jewish opinion, or were inattentive to the variety
of opinion in contemporary Jewish thought and scholarship. I
did not wish to be guilty of a similar offense in my study of contemporary christologies. I therefore requested of the Society
that it avail itself of the exceptional expertise of its members to
inform me as to which christologies they considered representative of contemporary Christian thought. I was particularly concerned that, in a time of great theological pluralism, I be
exposed to the full range of Christian teaching in this area. I
have limited this study to the thinkers the Society's consultants
suggested, though now that my project has been concluded I
feel a sense of personal loss that I did not investigate the views
of a right-wing Catholic or an Orthodox theologian. I wish now
to record my gratitude to Roger Shinn, Gordon Kaufman and
Carl Henry for their guidance, particularly for specifying what
they considered the basic writings of each thinker. These colleagues are in no way responsible for the errors of understanding or interpretation here, though I hoped to avoid such
mistakes by extending the bibliography they suggested. I also
benefitted from the Society's discussion of my paper and revised
and extended it accordingly. Naturally, the Society bears no responsibility for the views I express here. I would also like to

thank those who read this manuscript for the Hebrew Union College Press, particularly for the improvements they suggested in it: Jakob J. Petuchowski, Samuel Sandmel, Seymour Siegel and Wilfred Cantwell Smith. To the Chairman of the HUC Publications Committee, Michael A. Meyer, and to the Chairman *pro tem,* Herbert Zafren, for graciousness beyond the responsibilities of office, I remain indebted. My continuing thanks are offered to Dr. Paul M. Steinberg, Dean of the New York School of the Hebrew Union College–Jewish Institute of Religion, who on several occasions extended himself beyond his usual kind helpfulness to meet the special needs of preparing and revising this manuscript. My thanks too to Lawrence Raphael, Associate Dean of the New York School, and Frayda Ingber, its Registrar, for their assistance in seeing this project through the many stages of its completion. I am particularly grateful to Seymour Rossel for his literary review of the text and for his many sensitive suggestions for improving it.

II. Knox:
The Christ of Liberalism

Following its publication in 1947, John Knox's book, *On the Meaning of Christ,* was characterized as presenting a view of the Christ widely held by mainline Protestants in recent decades. While most of Knox's explication of the meaning of the Christ is thus familiar, it is nonetheless essential at the outset to present a rounded statement of what the Christ means to a thoughtful Christian. In Knox's exposition summarized below we confront the major terms and events, the affirmations and symbolic statements, the problems and speculations around which christology moves.

Jesus Christ is "what is most distinctive and most decisive in Christian life and faith" (p. 1*). God has made himself known in Christ (p. 16). The reality of Jesus Christ "just because it is a concrete reality is infinitely rich and complex and no simple or single category will suffice for an adequate description of it." These intersecting themes converge in him: the "event" (or series of events); the person at their center; the community in which the event transpired and which it created (p. 19). ". . . this central event must be thought of as including . . . the personality, life, and teaching of Jesus, the response of loyalty he awakened, his death, his resurrection, the coming of the Spirit, the faith with which the Spirit was received, the creation of the community" (p. 34). His whole life was significant but his crucifixion

* All references in this section are to *On the Meaning of Christ.*

10

and resurrection need to be seen as the most important events in it (pp. 38–39).

Knox discusses how the early Church transformed the Jewish expectation of the Messiah and understood Jesus to be its fulfillment. This, in turn, led on to the doctrine of God having become man in Jesus; and so to the two-nature formulas of Nicaea and Chalcedon (pp. 44ff and particularly p. 56). As a climax to this account, Knox quotes, with approval, Norman Pittenger's statement, "Jesus, is then, truly human; he is truly divine . . ." and adds *"The act of God which he is*—God has drawn near in Christ; He has visited and redeemed His people" (p. 58). While the resurrection "was a genuine occurrence" (p. 68), the Gospel miracles are a retrojection into the life of Jesus of what later was known to be his meaning (p. 80). Many other such dramatic matters recounted about him must also be considered "one place removed" from the event though they are part of "the story," which, as story, is now an indispensible part of the community appropriation of the event. The story is, therefore, true (pp. 86, 89). It teaches that man is alieniated from God but, through the life and death of Jesus, man is reconciled with God. As Jesus conquered sin for us, so he conquered death, was resurrected and now reigns with God.

The Gospels tell the story in narrative form and it thus may not have taken place as given in our text. However, its meaning is beyond challenge. "God is in fact our Redeemer from Sin and Death" (p. 92 and the context). The Christ creates the Church and there, to this day, the Spirit meets people (p. 99). He thus brings into being "a new people" (p. 102). ". . . upon the event, as the Christian is bound to see things, depends nothing less than the meaning of human history" (p. 112), for through it "God's purpose . . . will have been fulfilled . . . the creation in fact of the family of God . . ." (p. 113).

In one respect Knox is somewhat atypical of the other thinkers we shall discuss. Knox was a New Testament scholar rather than a theologian and so was more concerned with the problems raised by the Gospel accounts of the Christ than by what the creeds or other christological formulations say. The theologians studied below recognize that they must not violate the New Testament image of the Christ if they are to be authentic Christians, but they are primarily interested in the intellectual questions involved in asserting Jesus' Christ-hood.

Knox's presentation, for all its reasonableness, has a paradoxical character, making readers such as me ask in what way it is being addressed to them. On the one hand, Knox makes sweeping claims for the Christ. The event was "supremely authentic," "the revealing act of God," "supreme revelation . . . something of decisive importance for humanity really happened" (pp. 13, 14, 29, 35, 111). Yet Knox almost never presents these as claims for the reader to accept but only as descriptions of what he regularly calls "the common Christian faith." Many of the phrases given above are qualified by the modest article "a." On one of the few occasions when he uses the stronger specification, "*the* revealing act of God," he qualifies it by preceding it with the words "as *act* of God—or, if one prefers . . . the revealing act of God" (p. 29). He limits many of his assertions by putting them in the context of the community that believes them. ". . . if this is our faith . . ." ". . . as the Christian is bound to see things . . ." ". . . as Christian faith affirms . . ." (pp. 111, 113).

Morever, Knox settles some of the most crucial questions with regard to the Christ by posing rhetorical questions. Thus at the beginning of his presentation he inquires, "Can we deny that it [our knowledge of God] had its origin some way in Christ? . . . What does this mean if not that our religious life is what it is largely because a certain event occurred in Palestine nearly two thousand years ago?" (p. 4). And he argues that membership in the Church implies commitment to given beliefs. Thus, to be a Christian is to know that no evidence could come to light that would deny the historicity of Jesus (p. 37) and, out of the experience of the Spirit in the community, to know that Christ lives and thus was resurrected (p. 39). In the dispute with Judaism as to whether Christ is the Messiah, he concludes, "[the decision] will depend on one's point of view. There can be no questions about what will be the Christian's judgment. A member of the Christian community will, simply in virtue of the fact, see it [the transformation of the Messiah-expectation] as disclosure" (p.

32). Despite what seem like claims being made for the Christ, Knox is only explicating the faith of the Christian community.

It is not necessary to attribute Knox's limited form of address to the reader to the circumstance that his text was originally a set of lectures given to a Protestant seminary audience. We now have it before us as published for a broad public to read. Rather Knox has utilized a well-accepted modern method of studying religion and approached christology phenomenologically, that is, by explaining the inner life of a Christian believer. He thus makes a claim for its validity only upon those who stand beside him within this community of faith. He does not address himself to the lapsed believer, the uncertain believer, the searching semibeliever, much less the nonbeliever or one who believes in another faith. The phenomenological stance is often adopted today in religious discourse as one of the few ways we have of communicating the reality of faith to people who have grown up in a culture that values methodical doubt. Instead of trying to convince or persuade those who take a sceptical stand, one limits oneself to giving them an accurate representation of one's faith—while perhaps silently hoping that those who have now gained insight into it will be moved to acknowledge that they share it.

The phenomenological method has one severe limitation. Being strictly descriptive it calls for no response from those to whom its results are addressed. It only conveys information. The hearers may do with their new knowledge what they wish for no claim has been made on them. There is surely a need for such phenomenological communication in interreligious discussions. We are often misinformed about significant aspects of other religions and we are normally strangers to their inner life. Phenomenology can open another person's spirit to us—no small accomplishment indeed. One might appropriately respond to such a presentation by speaking of one's own faith and then perhaps explore some comparisons and contrasts between the two faiths. At an early level of acquaintance that is a useful procedure.

Recognizing this limit, I still think it fair to inquire to what extent Knox's Christ represents "the common faith" of contemporary Christianity. Note the difficulty Knox's goal imposed on him. Any effort to articulate a consensus of belief involves a step back from the rich mix of the shared and the disputed to an intuition of the unity underlying them. In omitting aspects of the faith he finds troubling, he may have left out of his christology what some believers consider essential and they will adjudge him a reductionist. In Knox's case there will be considerable argument over the appropriate criterion of christology. For him, that is not the person of the Christ, as it is for Karl Barth, or the New Testament writers, as it is for G. C. Berkouwer. Knox integrates the person and the community centered about him with what he calls the "event," a term of relatively wide meaning (pp. 27ff). He thus elevates a judgment about Christian experience, specifically his human sensibility, above the Christ or the New Testament. Barth and Berkouwer are explicit that such a procedure is unacceptable to them, and they consider such modernist approaches to the Christ inauthentic. Thus, though Knox says he is explicating the common basis of Christianity, it would be more accurate to describe his christology as what liberal Christians see themselves sharing with their more traditional coreligionists.

The Jewish analogue of this experience may be seen in the effort to articulate a meta-*halachic* basis for Jewish unity. That is to say, since Jews now differ widely on what constitutes proper observance of Jewish law (*halachah*), is it possible to find the continuing ground of Jewish community in a shared belief that undergirds the law? (Borowitz, 1973b, pp. 24f). What troubles Orthodox Jewish spokesmen in such discussions is apparently less whether such meta-*halachic* unity can be described than the legitimacy of the procedure, given the traditional Jewish priority of disciplined action over thought. Thus, the conflict between the views becomes intense when an effort is made by the non-Orthodox to claim *halachic* process, but guided by what the Orthodox consider to be a heterodox meta-*halachic* principle.†

A further question must be raised. Does Knox's statement

_____

† For a poignant example see the exchange between Hannah Parnes and Blu Greenberg, on the issue of abortion, *Sh'ma*, 5/81. This evoked a defense of the

of three decades or so ago express the common conviction of contemporary liberal Christians? Let us take as our test cases Knox's explanation of three matters that are central to classic Christianity and in serious dispute between Jews and Christians: the resurrection, "Chalcedon" (that is, the classic definition of the nature and person of the Christ given by this Council of 451 C. E.) and the uniqueness of the Christ event.

Knox affirms the resurrection as a real occurrence by link-ing it to the witnesses' experience that "the Spirit had come upon them" (p. 39). He continues, "and in our case too this con-viction is not the consequence of visual experiences reported in the Gospels and Epistles but of the presence of the Spirit in the community. The one remembered is still known . . . The one who lived and died—even he!—lives still; and it is possible still both to walk with him in the way and to know him in the break-ing of bread. This is the meaning of the resurrection in any sense that matters . . ." (p. 40). These words antedate the American debate over Rudolf Bultmann's demythologizing of the resurrection from a historical event to a consequence of the rise of the disciples' Easter faith, but seem to reflect the same idea. Because Christians know the reality of God's presence and forgiveness, they say that the resurrection is real, that is, that it occurred. For Knox the resurrection then seems to be the symbolic way Christians express the religious experience of God's love. But modern spirituality perceives God's gracious love in many places. Many Christians will therefore want to be explicit about their belief that the resurrection testifies as much about what happened to Jesus as it does about our experience. To what extent, then, does Knox's demythologized resurrection represent liberal christology today?

Similar questions may be raised about Knox's treatment of the Chalcedonian Creed's two-nature description of the Christ and the traditional claims made for his uniqueness. Knox ap-

---

legitimacy of non-traditional *halachah* by Seymour Seigel, 5/84, and an imme-diate Orthodox response, 5/89, that such *"halachah"* is not *halachah.* A similar series of rejoinders followed Mark S. Golub's liberal call for values to replace *halachah, Sh'ma* 6/106, which was rejected as inauthentically Jewish by Don Well 6/109 and Michael Asheri and David Haber 6/115.

proaches Chalcedon's statement about the Christ by deploring the shift from an original soteriological sense of his person to a metaphysical one. He comments, apparently with himself in mind, "a significant minority in the Church, then and since, has found [this doctrine of the Christ as simultaneously God and man] . . . either unintelligible or incredible" (p. 56). He says flatly of the creeds "because they are the symbols historically developed to express that meaning, they can never be replaced" (p. 57)—a statement which, were it being used to describe Judaism, would probably be considered the sort of "legalism" from which Christ had freed Christians, or at least most Protestants. To Knox, Chalcedon *et al.* "are authentic symbols of God's uniquely and supremely revelatory act in Christ . . . Christ is 'of one substance with the Father'; but the utmost, and inmost, it is given us to know God's 'substance' is that He is love . . ." (p. 57). By calling the Chalcedonian two-nature formula a "symbol," Knox demythologizes it. It raises the truth reference of God-manhood far beyond its denotation as a historical reality. It thereby also empties the two-nature formula of much of what people had taken to be its direct meaning. Chalcedon's assertion of Jesus as very God and very man now becomes something like Jesus is love as God is love. In a culture where love is a secular commonplace, this seems to me a thesis so easily susceptible to sentimentalization that it almost has no content. I wonder how many contemporary liberal Christians would find it an adequate statement of Jesus' divinity?

The logical consequence of such treatment of the resurrection and Chalcedon is the tacit admission by Knox that Jesus is unique only in his historicity as person (i.e., as all people are unique) or in the way he serves as a symbol for the Christian community. Note the qualifications in the following statements: "[that] we know Him so . . . does not shut out the possibility of other revelations although it is hard to see how the particular reality, the God and Father of our Lord Jesus Christ [*sic*, not simply "God" or "the Lord" or "the Almighty"] could be known elsewhere or otherwise than in and through Christ. But the common and all-important affirmation with which we start is not a dogmatic assertion that God has revealed Himself only in Jesus Christ, but the glad confession that He has revealed Himself there to us" (pp. 16–17).

In dispensing with the universal claims for the Christ, Knox thought himself to be expressing the common belief of liberal Christianity. Perhaps he did and perhaps this is still the position of liberal Christians, but in mood if not perhaps in content I wonder if nonfundamentalist Christians have not moved on to another attitude toward faith. In Knox's lectures liberal religion breathes confidence: Knox knows that he will get positive answers to his rhetorical questions. Without saying so, he hopes to persuade us to his faith by the appeal of his personal style—his moderation in judgment and in claim; his modest display of learning and his continual concern for simple piety; his devotion to the past yet his willingness to interpret it in terms of the human situation; his occasional display of personal faith and religious passion which, one may be certain, will never become an embarrassment. Knox seems to me a personal paragon of the liberal approach to religion. He is the sort of figure I found so appealing in liberal Judaism when I was young. And this moves me to ask, three tumultuous decades after he gave his lectures, how representative of liberal christology does he remain?

In the Jewish community much of the older liberalism still functions. Many a rabbi or layperson continues to think of revelation as human discovery; Torah as ethics or culture; chosenness as ethnic difference; and messianism as social betterment. But while the liberal language is heard and no clear doctrine has emerged to take its place, the spirit seems to have gone from it. The times have changed. Liberalism meant the accommodation of tradition to the modern world. With our civilization troubled if not collapsing, the liberal agenda seems outdated and even— the hardest blow—irrelevant. A post-liberal mood dominates the non-Orthodox Jewish community and provides much of the drive behind the revitalization of Orthodoxy (Borowitz, 1980). The fresh voices and interesting ideas of recent years have spoken in their accents. I wonder if the same social-spiritual conditions that brought about this situation have not affected the acceptability of Knox's Christ in contemporary liberal Christianity.

As important as these questions are, our inquiry must move beyond them, for we cannot afford to remain on the phenomenological level of interreligious discussion. It cannot take us much beyond a preliminary conversation. It enables us to surmount the ignorance that stands between us. But knowing each other better we realize that there is much about which we disagree. If we are to do more than identify such disputed topics we must move beyond phenomenological exchange. We need to find a way to explore each other's claim to truth and engage each other substantively, to the extent that it is possible. We shall not properly understand or respect one another until we move from communication to argument.

Such a suggestion makes many religionists anxious, and with good reason. The investment of self in central religious symbols is so great that a challenge to them is often taken personally and reacted to violently. Existentially, we often defend ourselves with high hostility against what we perceive as threats to the intellectual-spiritual ground of our existence, our faith. Historically, interreligious difference has often had horrifying consequences. Words like Crusade, Inquisition and holy war bring to mind some of the worst episodes in human behavior. If we are somewhat civilized about religious polemics today it is because many people do not take their beliefs very seriously, or because they prefer superficiality with agreement to the conflict that might accompany a probing spirituality. Such an attitude has no place in honest interreligious exchange. Not to take God seriously is blasphemy. To be religious is to affirm that nothing is more important to us than God, that our faith is the ground of our existence. We live or die by it. Hence while we may be willing to discuss, explain, interpret, modify, or develop our beliefs—and in extraordinary circumstances radically alter or change them—we will not trivialize them. People who take religion less seriously than that should not expect to be listened to carefully when they talk about it.

With so much at stake most moderns seek to avoid or soften

interreligious confrontation. Psychologically we prefer to be loved than argued with and to repress our hostility rather than have it exposed in the clash of convictions. Morally we desire peace and abhor what fanaticism has done and can do today. Theologically, we live in a world of pluralism, intradenominational as well as world-wide, and thus cannot be certain that our view is worth the possibility of alienating others. And socially we are trained to the democratic style where everything seems manageable if people will only talk it out and reach a compromise. This gives rise to the old liberal hope that communication itself will enable us to transcend difference: dialogue will bring the Messiah. Then the requirements of good "process" are falsely understood to constrain participants in a discussion from addressing the issues that sharply divide them or from expressing the depth of emotion they attach to them. Civility usurps the moral mandates of true communication and we come to know each other only as we are alike.

Despite risks, interreligious discussion needs at times to be interreligious debate. That is one way it shows its conviction that truth is ultimately one and validates its teaching that not everyone who claims to be a prophet is to be followed. There is an element of moral witness involved here as well.

In demonstrating how serious disagreement need not lead to the violation of one's antagonist, religionists would show how love of God properly becomes love of neighbor, thus serving as a valuable model for a sorely divided humanity. It would be a sign of spiritual growth indeed if, after all the bitter history of Christian-Jewish polemics, these faiths could find a mutually respectful way of rejoining the acrimonious issues that divide them.

One can adduce some positive theological reasons for respecting those who deny our truth and thus engaging them in friendly if vigorous exchange. Both Judaism and Christianity have given a high worth to personahood and individuality. Until recently these values were subordinated to their sense of certainty in their revelation. With the high moral worth moderns have put upon being true to one's own conscience, many theologians, including some of a quite conservative bent, acknowledge the virtue of not coercing unbelievers to accept one's own faith. Liberals can take this line of thought much further and admit that all human knowledge of God's truth is limited. For them, openness to the faith of others is a religious imperative. Pragmatically too we have all learned much about tolerance from our secular critics. Ever since the Enlightenment these critics have made great moral capital of the hatred fomented by the great religions. To benefit from their critique is not a capitulation to secularism. What in mere nature, human or physical, mandates genuine concern for an opponent? Our tolerance of difference stems rather from our recognition of the distance between human institutions and theologies, and God's kingdom and truth. God is so great that we may often find people have genuinely perceived God in what, on first sight, appear to us to be their odd religious notions. And if we agree with the existentialists that God is better known through persons than through doctrines, we will have genuine respect for the religious authenticity of those whose faith clashes with ours.

Only by directly confronting our deepest differences can we come to know one another fully. We are who we are as much by our divergence from one another as by our similarity. Paradoxical as it sounds, I do not think we properly comprehend our own religion until we see it in its distinctive divergence from other human faiths.

I think it important then that we move from the level of phenomenology to that of clashing truth-claims. William Christian has clearly distinguished between these forms of religious exchange (1972, pp. 17ff). His major interest is the logic by which protagonists of clashing beliefs might urge their opponents to agree with them. While much of Christian's universal analysis is helpful to us, special problems beset Christian-Jewish theological discussions. Christianity grows out of and relates to Judaism in ways radically different from Buddhism's emergence from Hinduism. Christianity claims to be a continuation of Judaism, including Hebrew Scripture in its Bible and citing it in the Gospels and Epistles it calls sacred. More importantly, Christianity has declared itself to be the fulfillment of Jewish faith, setting forth claims for Jesus that contradict Judaism. Jesus of Nazareth is the Messiah, the only Messiah, for though he transforms the Jewish expectation, his person, not any prophecy concerning his coming, is the standard of correct Messiahship. Jewish faith is, therefore, charitably put, self-limiting or, more severely, obsolete. Modern christologies, as they continue or alter the traditional claims made for the Christ, fix the exact nature of the theological difference between Christianity and Judaism. This is one good reason for a Jew to study them. They cannot, however, simply be analyzed in terms of William Christian's universal logic of competing truth-claims as applied so cogently by him to possible arguments between Judaism and Buddhism. In the Judeo-Christian engagement, the contradictions are organic in ways that keeps them from being universalizable.

We can clarify this unique relationship by noting that Judaism makes no counterclaims of equivalent importance to its faith. To be sure, Judaism insists that the Messiah has not come, but this assertion has more to do with the world than with the claims put forward on behalf of Jesus. He, like a number of others who aspired to be the Messiah, did not change the world and inaugurate God's rule on earth. These claimants so obviously do not fit Jewish messianic expectations that they have no special role in Jewish faith. When Jews in Christian lands have been pressed by Christian claims for Jesus' Messiahhood, they have responded to them. But the extensive literature of Jews who lived in Zoroastrian and Muslim countries clearly indicates that believing Jews have had no need to assert anything about Jesus.

Moreover, the truth Jews urge upon non-Jews is quite different from that of Christian evangelism. Judaism has long taught that non-Jews need not become Jews to know God, to serve God properly, or to achieve "a portion in the world-to-come," the messianic time. They need only be faithful to the covenant God made with Noah and his children (Gen. 8.20–9.19). As the rabbis generally understood it, that involves their keeping seven commandments. The Jewish counterpart to the universal lordship of Jesus Christ is not the authority of the Torah *as it applies to Jews* but, based on the Torah, the authority

of the covenant with "the Children of Noah."* In sum, while
Christians have traditionally claimed that all Jews ought to be
Christians, Jews have said only that Christians (and other non-
Jews) ought to live by the seven commandments enjoined upon
them under the covenant of the Children of Noah.†

There is another special factor that colors any Jewish-Christian debate: anti-Semitism. Christianity did not originate hatred
of the Jews but it carried and abetted it wherever it went. James
Parkes, Malcolm Hay, Ed Flannery and, most recently, Rosemary Ruether have described this sad situation to the point
where it requires no further elaboration by me. I only wish to
point out that Ruether calls christology "the key issue" in Christian anti-Semitism and connects the two so intimately that she
wonders, "Is it possible to say 'Jesus is Messiah' without implicitly saying at the same time 'the Jews be damned'?" (1974, p.
246).

Jews, then, see a special condition devolving upon Christians who undertake to speak of their faith to us. They must not
be uninformed or insensitive to what has been done to Jews over
the centuries in the name of the Christ and to what extent this
deposit of hatred, now secularized and politicized, continues to
draw strength from Christian teaching and silence. They also
ought to know in advance—and I cannot emphasize it strongly

---

* The "full" Torah, the Oral as well as the Written teaching, is directed only to
Jews. Note how this would change the oppositions set up by Christian (1972,
pp. 3ff and 50). This is meant as no disparagement of Christian's work which
I highly esteem. His concern is formal-logical rather than historical-substan-
tive. Hence he regularly disclaims doctrinal authenticity for his various propositions of faith so that he may focus exclusively on the consequences of
opposing certain possible affirmations to each other. I offer these references
only to show how, if one were not careful about the two levels of authority asserted by Jewish faith, one might find opposition where none existed or a different sort from that which Judaism has understood to exist.

† The Jewish view of what would happen to non-Jews when the Messiah came is
only one of a number of variables in the open, unregulated but discouraged
realm of eschatological speculation. One can find references to all the nations
being destroyed at the final judgment, or their becoming Jews, or maintaining
their identity. On the Jewish view of non-Jews in general and Christians in particular, see Katz (1962).

enough—that most Jews evaluate claims for the Christ in terms of Christian treatment of the Jews. When a Christian says "Christ" a sensitive Jew begins listening for anti-Semitic overtones.* "Christ brings a religion of love." "But how have you treated the Jews?" "Christ redeems us from our old sinfulness so we may live in freedom." "But how have you treated the Jews?" "Christ teaches us that we must be people-for-others." "But how have you treated the Jews?" More, the Jewish counterquestion must be put into the present tense. We have been so hurt by past Christian teaching and practice, we are so worried now about the terms on which the world (still so strongly influenced by Christian opinion) will permit us to survive, that our first question to any Christian is likely to be "What do you believe is your Christian obligation to the Jews and what will you be doing about it?"

Perhaps I have set too high a condition for the discussion of Jewish-Christian differences to continue. If so, I am sorry, for I think there is much we need to learn from one another. But I cannot withdraw the condition. This is one implication of my comment above that the conventions of positive communication may not displace the realities of content.

I cannot leave it at that. Christianity's relation to anti-Semitism is a personal matter to me. None of my immediate family was killed in the Holocaust, but among my most formative preteen memories are the appearance in our small Midwestern Jewish community of German refugee children. I still tremble physically when at some Jewish get-together a sleeve slides back to show a tatooed concentration camp number. And again and again in recent years people and institutions whom I trusted to understand Jews, in part because they said they were concerned to right the wrongs Jews have suffered at Christian hands, have shown insensitivity to Jewish pain. This makes me fear that our society's ostensible rejection of anti-Semitism has not yet overcome generations of history and social conditioning.

---

* No wonder the Jewish community usually considers Jews who become Christians to be so burdened by self-hate that their enthusiastic acceptance of Jewish form or communal obligation is dismissed as inauthentic.

The most critical matter in Jewish life these days is the survival of the state of Israel in a way that ensures the vitality of Jewish existence on the covenanted land. That may seem a political problem, but it is also a theological one from the vantage of Jewish faith. God's Covenant with the Jews is made with an ethnic group not a church. An integral part of that Covenant is the promise of the land of Israel, on which that Covenant is to be worked out socially and individually. In the present historical-political situation, to effectuate that Covenant in the land of Israel involves having a Jewish state. And in this post-Holocaust generation, the fate of that state carries incalculable consequences for all of world Jewry. It may help to remember Buber's hybrid coinage for describing Jewish faith: he said it is properly lived on a "theo-political" plane. I do not understand this to mean that the state of Israel is beyond criticism or that no one else has rights to the Holy Land or that there is really only one side to the political problems there. I do mean that it is at the point of differences of opinion—particularly when there is a clash of real needs or desires—that one's true feelings regularly appear. Often in reading or talking to Christian colleagues about the problems of the state of Israel vis-à-vis the survival of the Jewish people, I find them unconsciously reverting to an old, inner sense that the Jews are dispensable now that the Christ has come. So while they may personally like Jews, they do not see that as Christians they ought to have any special concern for the welfare of the Jews. Sometime I believe the specific social or political attitudes that they then have are simple human decisions, wrong, I think, but authentically made. Often I find in them a modern version of classic Christian anti-Semitism, enlightened beyond physical violence (but what of the Germans?) yet nonetheless destructive of my people. Readers of this study should take into account these subjective concerns that I have brought to the engagement of the differences to be discussed and which will animate my reactions to any response they may wish to make to what I have written here.

III. Berkouwer, Barth and Pannenberg: Modern Claims for the Traditional Christ

The christologies of G. C. Berkouwer and Karl Barth seem to me to present the classic assertions of Christian faith, though in a modern form. Israel's expected Messiah came in the person of Jesus of Nazareth. Through his life, death, resurrection and glorification, it has become clear to those who, by the grace of God have faith in Jesus Christ, that he is the unique means by which people truly know God. Jesus Christ is thus the standard by which we judge all religious truth. For Barth this primarily means his person. While the New Testament text is the best and indispensible witness to him, we must subordinate its language about him to the person to whom it testifies. Christians worship the Christ, not the New Testament text (Come, 1963, pp. 171–172). Berkouwer would agree on the centrality of the Christ but places greater emphasis upon the specific words used about the Christ, for he considers the New Testament text inerrant. Thus on the debate over christologies he writes, "yet the message of Scripture will be the sole, final, and real viewpoint in the midst of all confusion" (1965, p. 10). For Berkouwer it is true that Jesus was born of a virgin, is now in heaven reigning with God as our Lord and will return in glory to complete the working out of God's kingdom. Faith knows him, in all of this, to have been true man and true God, and to have had this double nature as the four negatives of the creed of Chalcedon indicated, without "division, separation, mixture or change" (1954, passim, e.g., p. 92). Such incarnation was unknown to Israel and

25

the form, content and two-stage nature of his Messiahship were unanticipated. Now that he has been revealed in full stature, he, in fulfilling and transforming what was expected, is the criterion by which all Messianic expectation is to be evaluated. Being man and God simultaneously, he was uniquely able to mediate between a sinful humanity and God. Through his life and especially by his death, he reconciled humankind with God. People are now called upon to accept freely, in faith, what has been done for them in the Christ and, by this response to the grace of God, to be saved. (The emphasis on salvation by God's grace alone is so strong in Berkouwer and Barth that the absence of a traditionalist Catholic christology was felt, though undoubtedly there would be far more convergence than divergence.)

One does not gain this truth by reasoning it out for oneself but by responding to what God has done for each person in the Christ. One comes to faith only by God's grace. Barth had so long and strenuously asserted humankind's impotence to comprehend or define or delimit God that his eventual treatment of God's own humanity came as something of a turn in his theology. He now acknowledged that having given priority in his thought to a polemic against liberal interpretations of Christianity, he may have overemphasized the sovereignty of God. In the Christ, we know God as man as well as God (1960, pp. 37ff). Barth can then laugh at his and his colleagues' use in the past of such phrases as "'wholly other,' breaking in upon us 'perpendicularly from above,' . . . 'infinite qualitative distinction'" (p. 42). Nonetheless "there is no question of denying the change" Barth wished to make from liberal thought (p. 41). Thus, consistent with Barth's "Christo-monism," even God's humanity and its implications for human existence are christologically derived (p. 46). Barth's turn to the human side of the God-man equation does not invalidate his traditionalism. All of the familiar themes of Barth's theology, the divine sovereignty and initiative, human subordination, the grace-faith equation, remain centered in the person of the Christ, who is available to people only through God-given faith.

Berkouwer is similarly polemical in denying that human reason, in any unaided form, is adequate to the understanding

of Christian truth. The incarnation "does not have a single in-
tracosmic analogy . . . which can make it at all comprehensible.
In the absolute sense of the word it is the mystery of God"
(1954, p. 299). So he agrees with Barth's view that "Revelation
always takes place in such a manner that without faith one can
never distinguish it from that which is non-revelational" (p.
337). "Scripture inseparably connects the true knowledge of
Christ's office with salvation. Our own flesh and blood does not
yield this knowledge either. It is possible . . . only by the Father's
revelation . . . " (1965, p. 10). ". . . this 'beholding' of his glory is
not a matter of course to anyone [a footnote here refers specifically to Jews] who observes his appearance, but it is a seeing by
faith after one's eyes have been opened for the mystery . . . " (p.
89). "It is evident that only by the light of revelation can a complete misunderstanding of Christ's suffering be avoided" (p.
148). So the resurrection "is a historical fact which must be believed with the heart" (p. 181; many other citations could be giv-
en). Berkouwer will also argue, in this case against Barth's
reduction of the virgin birth and the empty tomb to a "sign,"
that all these matters are "made known to us as part of an *indi-
visible totality*" (p. 106). One must accept them all as true or reject them all.

    Though the substance of his christology seems traditional,
Wolfhart Pannenberg dissents radically from Barth and Berkouwer with regard to the grounds on which one comes to know
the Christ (1968, pp. 33ff). He is, of course, an opponent of
Christian liberalism, arguing for example that the existentialists
are wrong when they seek to base belief on contemporary experience. For Pannenberg faith must be "based entirely on what
happened in the past . . . faith primarily has to do with what Jesus *was*" (p. 28). At the same time he rejects Barth's approach
and does christology "from below" (pp. 35ff), overcoming the
difficulty by moving logically from Jesus' humanity to his divinity by arguing for the historicity of the resurrection (pp. 53ff).
Pannenberg contends that "In view of the age of the formulated
traditions used by Paul and of the proximity of Paul to the
events the assumption that appearances of the resurrected Lord
were really experienced by a number of members of the primi-

tive Christian community and not perhaps freely invented in the course of later legendary development has good historical foundation" (p. 91). Pannenberg has introduced no special standards of historical judgment and made no appeal to a unique realm of experience. He has only insisted that the dogmatic naturalism of most academic methods of studying history has no more a priori claim upon us than does dogmatic religion. We learn what *can* happen in history by consulting reasonable evidence about what *did* happen in history (pp. 98–99). The historicity of the resurrection appears so evident to Pannenberg and it so firmly establishes the basic propositions of Christian faith that he often is quite critical of the use of other aspects of scripture or of other intellectual arguments to support a given tenet of faith. Knowing that the resurrection really occurred, Pannenberg has a sure and unambiguous basis for Christian belief. He therefore has no need to defend any argument that he considers dubious.

Jewish thinkers respond to these christologies with little difference of opinion.* The traditional christologies arouse a rather traditional Jewish reaction, many of whose themes go back to the earliest Jewish arguments with Christianity. In the Jewish view humanity does not need a mediator between itself and God, regardless of its sinfulness. As Ezekiel 18 makes perfectly plain to Jewish eyes, God has no interest in condemning sinners but only asks that they "turn," that is, return to God. When they do so, God gladly accepts the "turning" and is reconciled with the sinners so that they live. The God of Judaism so loves the world that atonement is always available if people will only "turn." For much of the Bible and for Rabbinic Judaism "turning" is a personal act and does not require a priest, a sacrifice or a liturgical rite. Of course the Torah provides for a Day of Atonement with highly structured Temple rites and a fast. That seems to be the communal culmination of what many Bible authors consider a universal everyday practice. The doctrine of "turning" is clearly a central part of the rabbis' picture of God's relation to humanity. They fixed the content of the Eighteen

---

* For a previous discussion by me of Barth as theologian, see Borowitz (1965, pp. 44ff).

Benedictions, a liturgy whose origins are in the time of Jesus or before, and those required daily prayers contain this petition: "Turn us, O Father, to Your Torah; draw us near, O King, to Your service; bring us back to Your presence through a complete turning. We bless You, Adonai, who desires turning." (My translation. The overtones of the final verb, "desires," *rotzeh*, are "delights in," "accepts," "wills.")

Judaism obviously has a high regard for humankind's capacity to right its disturbed relationship with God. This is not to be equated with the modern humanistic notion that sin is essentially a matter of human error and does not involve God. In the Jewish tradition confidence in humanity's power is balanced by a dependence on God. Thus, the stated daily prayer beseeches God's help in achieving a proper turning. One prays in confidence because one knows, as the text concludes, that this is what God desires. In my theological language, the Covenant relationship implies that God will forgive and bear with the human partner.

From the Jewish viewpoint, traditional Christianity's view of humanity—certainly as seen in Protestant thinkers who emphasize that God's grace alone effects reconciliation—derogates our power to act on our own behalf. In Barth and Berkouwer this problem surfaces in what seem to Jewish eyes the intricate arguments created to show why people must actively seek faith though it is given by God's grace alone. (For a good example see Berkouwer's chapter on "Election and the Preaching of the Gospel" [1960, pp. 218ff]). Partly their attitude derives from the Church's commitment to preaching whose nature seems designed to draw forth a human response. Surely another reason for their not permitting us to be utterly passive while awaiting God's grace is that people can do acts of religious significance, in this case, their part in the gaining of faith. To a Jew this seems a grudging admission of what ought to be a major theme in the service of God.

Hebrew scripture teaches that people can do what God commands—only a cruel God would have given an undoable law. Its concomitant teaching is that when one has sinned, one can turn back to God. Judaism sees the major activity of the religious life as having two aspects. In doing commandments humanity finds the proper expression of its covenant partnership. In the act of turning, we rely on God's Covenant faithfulness to renew our relationship in response to what we have done and because that is what God truly wants from us. Believing Jews seek no mediator though they still await the Messiah.

Neither Barth nor Berkouwer seeks to prove that Jesus is the Messiah. Rather, since this is a matter of faith, they begin with this knowledge and see its truth confirmed in many ways. Jews perceive things differently. They know the biblical texts about the coming of the Messiah, for these hopes were born of Jewish experience and stated in the Jewish tongue. They speak of peace and of justice, of humankind living in harmony and nature and humanity restored to a concord they have not known since Eden. By contrast, the present world, as Buber put it, is unredeemed. To Jews that proves that the Messiah has not come. We find it odd to hear that he has come but must come again. We do not know such a Messianic expectation and it seems to us that nothing much changed with his first coming. If anything the long Christian wait for the consummation of the Messiah's rule indicates to us that only one coming, the one that has not yet occurred, is critical to the inauguration of God's kingdom on earth.

Christians can persevere in faith until the second coming, because the resurrection proves Jesus was the Messiah. This matter raises again what, to Jews, seems the curious Christian logic of getting faith as against finding faith. For Barth and Berkouwer the resurrection is a divine mystery, one whose truth can only be gained by faith in the Christ which is a gift of God. Yet those who do not acknowledge the Christ bear responsibility for their state. The Jews, for rejecting Jesus as the Messiah and denying his resurrection, are a model of willful blindness and faithlessness. (On Pannenberg's historical approach to this theme, see below.)

Jews have felt there was no good reason to believe Jesus was resurrected. Had he died and then been given life in some eschatological fashion, they do not think their forebears would have utterly ignored or repressed such an event. Yet rabbinic literature is silent on the subject. While most of our sources were compiled decades later than Jesus, some echo of so extraordinary an event should still sound in them. So much else, of so heterodox a character, is found there that Jews find this absence of contemporary corroboration telling.

One may well wonder on what basis Jews still believe the Messiah will come since people are so evil and he tarries so long. They do so out of their living experience that the Covenant remains in force and their faith that God's promise will not fail. If there is a Jewish equivalent to the resurrection as a basis for enduring in faith it is the "resurrection" of the Jewish people. We have often been condemned to death—once before our own eyes—yet we live. Theologically, the survival of the Jews in unflagging religio-historic devotion, despite unending trials, is our sure sign of the continuing validity of the Covenant, whose climax is the coming of the Messiah.

That is hardly a rational faith, yet to a Jew there seems a qualitative difference between the level of credulity demanded of a Jew and of a Christian. To us, the Christian version of the relations between God and humankind seems far more intense and extraordinary than we experience it. God is so distant from humanity and it is so impoverished in relation to God, that a mediator is needed to reconcile them. Jesus cannot be a Jewish *hasid*, a "pietist," preaching repentance and the approach of God's kingdom; he must be seen as the Messiah who transformed Jewish messianic expectation. He died without inaugurating God's kingdom but he was resurrected and will come again. Until then he is most immediately known in the Church and its sacraments. But the Jewish sense that Christianity makes extraordinary demands on the believer is best exemplified by the doctrine of the incarnation, that Jesus was God enfleshed, true God and true man, at one and the same time. That is a scandal to all non-Christian monotheists. When Jews hear that a Church Father once said "I believe because it is absurd" then they, ignoring Tertullian's meaning or the theological status of this teaching, agree with his problem but not his conclusion. Jews find the two-nature doctrine of the Christ, as so much else in Christianity, "too much" to believe; the surd is too great for them. If Christian faith is a gift from God, as Barth and Berkouwer do not tire of telling us, then God, apparently, does not give it to many Jews.

By contrast, the fundamental assertion of Jewish faith is that God gave the Torah to the Jewish people and chose them alone to receive it. Such a belief involves a miraculous act and lays claim to historical uniqueness. To the Jewish believer, it requires a qualitatively different act of assent than do the virgin birth, the incarnation, the resurrection, the ascension and the real presence of the Christ in the Eucharist. The gift of the Torah to the Jews seems only a special case of revelation, an activity that devout Christians and Jews usually do not class with God's special changes of the natural order. Only one other miracle plays a part in Jewish faith—God's splitting the Sea of Reeds for the Israelites at the Exodus, an event recalled in our daily liturgy. That is as wondrous and mysterious as Jewish belief sees human history. Nothing central to traditional Jewish piety seems to us as distant from our everyday experience as are the claims Christianity makes for Jesus as the Christ.

Perhaps this intuition accounts for the odd place Christians have under Jewish law, though *halachic* reasoning customarily deals with legal not theological considerations. In Torah law as developed by the rabbis, the world is divided into two social categories, the Jews and "the nations." As a matter of cultural experience, the nations were assumed to be idolators. It created something of a problem to Jewish law when Christianity appeared and converted many of the nations. In due course, despite its use of icons and images, despite its doctrines of the incarnation and the trinity, the legal sages could not conscientiously classify it as idolatry. (Katz, 1962, traces this development.) They then created a special legal category for Christians. While the "association" (*shituf*) with God of any person or name other than God's own was forbidden to Jews, it was now ruled permissible when done by "the nations." Hence Christianity, which "associates" Jesus with God, was granted a certain legitimacy in Jewish law. Technically the law considers Christians still part of "the nations." But though they are in the classification of "idolaters," they worship the true God, albeit with "association." I see here a reflection of Judaism's ambivalence to Christianity. It is a religion of ex-idolaters who worship God but came to it in a way that, though permitted them, retains overtones of idolatry. Most modern Jewish thinkers attribute the seemingly extreme quality of belief demanded by Christianity to its syncretism of Jewish faith with Hellenistic and other Near Eastern idolatry, symbolism and myth. While an occasional non-Orthodox Jewish spokesman has suggested that Christianity is fully as true (for Christians) as Judaism—Franz Rosenzweig is the most famous case—I know of no Orthodox Jewish thinker who has taken such a stand.

The foregoing response will mean nothing to Barth and Berkouwer. They expected some such incredulity from nonbelievers. Indeed their theologies are formed in anticipation of such arguments and operate so as to render them meaningless. Christ is the criterion of all truth and value. No one may presume to stand in judgment over him. Faith alone reveals him as occupying this position so it is to be assumed non-Christians will not accept his sovereignty. Until they come to faith, one can only preach to them the good news of Christ's coming and pray that the Spirit will awaken them to faith. Christians such as Barth and Berkouwer feel an obligation to make the truth known to nonbelievers, but they do not expect to learn anything from them about ultimate reality for that is given only in the Christ. When believers like Barth and Berkouwer become involved with the world and its cultures, they do so to understand the common ways of unredeemed humanity, hoping thereby that they may better understand how to preach the Gospel and make converts for Christ.

I have no objection to people wanting to make converts to their belief. If one has confidence in the truth of one's faith and finds great personal fulfillment or social value in it, one will naturally want others to share it and join in the work it entails. Talking to such a committed person involves the risk of having to give up one's previously held belief. We submit ourselves to a similar challenge in any significant intellectual exchange and do so out of a passion for truth and a desire to learn as much of it as we can. More is at stake in interreligious discussions because our lives hinge on the outcome. Yet the risk of conversion is worth taking for what we are likely to learn from engagement with another religion should speak to us most profoundly about ourselves as well as about them.

What is deeply objectionable to me is a one-way discussion. Your dialogue partner expects you to respond in full personal openness but remains closed to anything you might say. Your contributions to the exchange are discounted in advance. Only your willingness to convert is of interest. This is an immoral engagement, a violation of the mutuality implicit in the convenant of conversation. I believe in the truth I bring to our exchange about our faiths. I have based my life on it. If you will not listen to what I believe true in the same way you expect me to listen to what you have to say to me, then you have no genuine respect for me. I am, at best, something like a child who needs an adult to point out what is right; at worst I am so incompetent without your help that you have no hesitation in manipulating me into a conversion. In any case, you do not consider me a real person, capable of knowing the truth without you and therefore possibly able to teach you something you now do not know. Under such circumstances, do not ask me to talk to you seriously. I do not wish to surrender my soul as a condition of dialogue.

We have come to an intriguing impasse. Traditional Jews and traditional Christians would seem to have much in common. The both read the Hebrew scripture and believe that God acts (as in giving the Torah); and does so unexpectedly (keeping the Jews in Egyptian slavery for over 400 years); indeed, doing acts unique in history (as at Mt. Sinai). Yet if the Christ is the standard of all things, including scripture, and faith is the prerequisite of understanding him properly, what can Jews say meaningfully about the Christ to Christians like Barth and Berkouwer? And how can one engage in interfaith disputation with them?

We had sought to move beyond phenomenological religious exchanges to the discussion of our differences. Now it is clear that without some common frame of discourse, the diverse faiths cannot be significantly set over against one another. Note that in this instance the two faiths have an extensive common language, and though there may be differences of opinion as to the meaning of given terms, one would have expected that this would make possible communication in depth. However, in the exclusivity of the faith proclaimed by Barth and Berkouwer all hope of finding a common ground with non-Christians is shattered. Were there some genuine overlap between the two faiths under consideration—a common concept of the Messiah or an agreement on how to read scripture—the opposing faiths might then engage each other in the other's terms. When, however, God's truth is proclaimed in so absolutistic a fashion as in the christologies of Barth and Berkouwer, no such debate is possible. We are thrown back to the phenomenological level of discussion and are limited to the virtues it offers us.

By contrast, Pannenberg's assertion that the resurrection of the Christ is a historical event in the common, academic sense of the term, makes it possible to discuss our differences.† Pannenberg's argument for his faith is based on a separation of the empty tomb traditions from the resurrection appearances (1968, pp. 88–89). About the latter, he says, "the historical question of the appearances of the resurrected Lord is concentrated completely in the Pauline report, Cor. 15: 1–11" (p. 89). Pannenberg is, as often, quite critical of all other texts dealing with the resurrection. "The appearances reported in the Gospels, which are not mentioned by Paul, have such a strongly legendary character that one can scarcely find a historical kernel of their own in them. Even the Gospel's reports that correspond to Paul's statements are heavily colored by legendary elements, particularly by the tendency toward underlying the corporeality of the appearances" (p. 89). Pannenberg gives credence to the Pauline report first because "it is very close to the events themselves" (p. 90). Second, he considers Paul to be using "formulations coined previously . . . not . . . a possibly inaccurate memory, but he appeals to a formulated tradition . . . [that] must have reached back to the first five years after Jesus' death" (p. 90). He thus concludes, "In view of the age of the formulated traditions used by Paul

---

† I shall not discuss any other aspect of Pannenberg's christology. His argument for the historicity of the resurrection seems his most distinctive contribution in this area and his other affirmations about the Christ, which are substantively traditional, are based upon its facticity.

and of the proximity of Paul to the events, the assumption that appearances of the resurrected Lord were really experienced by a number of members of the primitive Christian community and not perhaps freely invented in the course of later legendary development has good historical foundation" (p. 91). So he cannot take seriously comparative religious data on dying and rising gods as the basis of this Church tradition (p. 91), and he rejects the dogmatic notion that the laws of nature do not allow for a resurrection (p. 98). Moreover, the explanation of the resurrection traditions on a psychological basis "have failed to date" (p. 96). In spite of Jewish apocalyptic expectations "Jesus' death exposed the faith of his disciples to the most severe stress. One could hardly expect the production of confirmatory experiences from the faith of the disciples that stood under a burden . . . [hence] the improbability of the assumption that people who came from the Jewish tradition would have conceived of the beginning of the events connected with the end of history for Jesus alone without compelling reasons. The primitive Christian news about the eschatological resurrection of Jesus . . . is . . . something new . . . " (p. 96). Further, the argument from the number of the appearances and their temporal distribution as due to psychological "chain reaction" is invalid. For example, "the appearance to five hundred brethren cannot be a secondary construction . . . because Paul calls attention precisely here to the possibility of checking his assertion by saying that most of the five hundred are still alive" (p. 97). Any competent historian must also ask what "events . . . led to the emergence of primitive Christianity" (p. 97). His understanding of what might happen in history will naturally affect his interpretation. If he believes in the possibility of an apocalyptic resurrection, he must consider, in the absence of a good alternate explanation, whether this is not the basis of the events here. "Thus the resurrection of Jesus would be designated as a historical event in this sense: If the emergence of primitive Christianity, which, apart from other traditions, is also traced back by Paul to appearances of the resurrected Jesus, can be understood in spite of all critical examination of the tradition only if one examines it in the light of the eschatological hope for a resurrection from the dead, then that which is so designated is a historical event, even if we do not know anything more particular about it. Then an event that is expressible only in the language of the eschatological expectation is to be asserted as a historical occurence" (p. 98).

Pannenberg has developed his case in terms of academic historical judgment though without its frequent covert dogmatic positivism. His findings might equally well be evaluated by Christian or Jewish scholars, excepting those liberals who are dogmatically antiresurrectionist. Furthermore, open-spirited secular historians could also participate in such a discussion as equals. Should such investigators agree that the resurrection had occurred, I find it difficult to believe that such an "is" (had happened) would not reasonably entail an "ought" (to believe). This is the potential importance of the facticity of the resurrection, a matter whose significance has often been discredited by Christian thinkers following the lead of Rudolf Bultmann. Against traditionalists like Barth and Berkouwer, Pannenberg considers the nonhistorical proclamation of christology unduly solipsistic. It prevents engaging nonbelievers with the distinctive teachings of Christianity and limits the Christian to preaching to them. Pannenberg hopes that by arguing for the truth of the Christ from a common intellectual ground, thoughtful people will see the truth of Christianity insofar as it is in a person's power to do so. He seeks to demonstrate the historicity of the resurrection as a means of bringing the world to faith in the Christ.

There is no distinctive Jewish response to Pannenberg's argument. There does not need to be, for the question raised is a neutral one: does the evidence Pannenberg presented justify the historical conclusion he reached? In the years since Pannenberg's argument became widely known in the United States it has not won wide acceptance among Christian theologians or academic historians. That cannot be ascribed to the positivism of the times, for this was the period of the decline of the death of God movement and a new openness to religious experience. The difficulty inheres in the argument. A community tradition that goes back to some years after Jesus' death, even if they are few, tells us only what the Church had come to believe about that death. It is only indirect testimony about what actually happened, from which in due course that tradition emerged. Similarly, Paul's testimony about people still living who had shared the visions indicates only that resurrection traditions were still alive. It does not tell us much about their historical reliability. Despite Pannenberg's rejection, the alternative explanation seems far more adequate. Though he agrees that the appearances were "visions," he denies that they can be explained psychologically. He considers the strain Jesus' death placed on the disciples a reason for their not creating a new doctrine rather than an impetus to it. He gives no credence to the religious (and social) psychological phenomenon, the will-to-believe, or to the sort of radical transformations of religious faith that frequently follow religious crises. He admits that groups have myth-making and legend-developing powers and that these were present in the early Church. He does not see that they could have a major factor in enabling the disciples to meet the trauma of Jesus' death. Moreover, while it might be strange to Jews of the first century that an eschatological resurrection had occurred, it was not as unthinkable an idea as Pannenberg makes out. There were living traditions that God had taken Enoch and Elijah bodily to heaven. If we may assume later Rabbinic traditions reflect earlier opinions, these biblical events were associated with the anticipated Messianic resurrection. Hence Jesus' resurrection as an eschatological event was not so inconceivable in the first century Judean community that it could not possibly have originated in the disciples' imagination.

The balance of the argument is now revised. The opponents see the likelihood of the psychological factor as sufficiently great that they must deny the legitimacy of taking the early traditions of a resurrection as proof of its having occurred. Evidence of a far more persuasive kind than Pannenberg offers would be required to shift the historical judgment from such a psychological explanation of the resurrection traditions. I am not certain whether it is sectarian to suggest that there is a substantial imbalance between what Pannenberg seeks to prove and the evidence he offers for it. Historians are asked to accept a unique, decisive, incursion of God into history and, as a likely result of that judgment, radically redirect their lives. The most extraordinary and significant event of all time is to be given historical status on the basis of a tradition circulating among enthusiasts of a young religious community as reported by a writer who accepted their faith a few years earlier on the basis of a vision that took place as part of a dramatic reversal of situation accompanied by unusual psychological side-effects.

These counterclaims convince me but they surely do not foreclose further discussion on this matter. A good deal might yet be fruitfully learned from discussing with Pannenberg and like-minded non-Jews the special problems of historical evidence for religious occurrences; how one is to deal with the necessary intertwining of interpretation and fact in religious historical judgments; what constitutes an appropriate ration of evidence to conclusion when consequences of cosmic significance are at stake; what a reasonable nonpositivistic view of history entails; and what, in general, is each faith's view of history and human destiny.

Despite this rejection of the Pannenberg proposal, its availability for discussion helps us to see other aspects of the structure of interreligious discussion. For example, Pannenberg's discussion of the historicity of the resurrection illustrates the importance of distinguishing traditionalist believers from liberals within a given faith and conducting debate only with thinkers who operate on a similar level. Pannenberg required that historians who dealt with this topic be open to the possibility that a resurrection might occur. Were they not, the issue would be foreclosed as a matter of "proper" methodology and no historical investigation could ever take place. Some historians would insist that the normal operation of nature must be the criterion of our judgment as to what can happen historically. They apply that rule to Judaism and insist that God's unique act of giving the Torah at Sinai must be understood in terms that reasonably conform to our usual range of experience. Thus they would reinterpret the Sinai experience as a convocation conducted by a charismatic personality under the impact of the Exodus and thus understood by people of that time to be a unique act of God. What the Torah describes as God's act of unparalleled self-revelation is historically translated into a natural human happening, whose religiosity is explained in terms of people's consciousness of it. Baldly put, traditionalist versions of a faith are divided from liberal ones by the emphasis on God's act as against human experience.

Without doubt there are special virtues to be found in each of these approaches to a religion. Traditionalists feel validated by their sense of authenticity in the received doctrines of their faith. Though they may permit the form in which their belief is presented to change somewhat, they measure religious truth primarily in terms of its conformity with their past. Liberals, on the other hand, authenticate their spiritual stance in the integration of their belief with the general human knowledge of their time. While they may want to continue a tradition, they limit the demands the past may make on the central insights of the contemporary human consciousness. In our time, the central issue dividing the two groups is whether God or humankind is essentially the creator of religion. Obviously, the terms traditionalist and liberal are imprecise. Many thinkers overlap the definitions given above, and we have recently seen the emergence of what may be called post-liberals (of whom, more below). Despite those limitations, utilizing the terms "traditionalist" and "liberal" helps clarify some important logical features of interreligious discourse.

Traditionalists and liberals have different standards of truth. From a philosophical point of view, theirs is an epistemological disagreement. (From the traditionalists' view, it is a division over faith, for faith acknowledges no extrinsic principle of religious validation including philosophic structures of what people can and cannot know.) Within a religion as between religions, the debate between traditionalists and liberals ultimately reduces itself to a disagreement over how one is to know what is true. Is tradition (centered about God) reasonably independent of modern thought or does contemporary experience (centered about human experience) fundamentally determine what we should believe?

This distinction indicates how a category-error can easily cause interreligious discussion to fail. For a liberal of one faith (e.g., me) to criticize a traditionalist of another faith (e.g., Barth) or vice versa, is, properly speaking, not to have an interreligious discussion at all. It is rather to criticize a faith being described in the terms of one epistemology by a differing epistemology. To dispute Barth's christology because of its unscientific sense of reality is not to challenge Barth's Christianity but his traditionalist way of speaking of religion. The fundamental difference involved is not between the content of the two faiths, which one would take to be the proper substance of interreligious discussions, but between a liberal and a traditional way of apprehending religious truth. We must not confuse the category of the form of a proper theology with the substance of a religious faith.

In the case of the resurrection, there is as good as no difference between liberal Jews and liberal Christians in evaluating the adequacy of traditionalist Christian arguments for its historicity. The same is true of a whole range of traditional claims for the Christ. Liberal Christians reject them because, in one sophisticated formulation or another, modern people do not think that way and require their faith to be expressed in other categories. Liberal Jews, utilizing similar human criteria, would find the arguments of Christian liberals persuasive. But the disagreement of the liberal Jews with traditional Christians is not essentially because of the Judaism of the liberal Jews but because of their liberalism, i.e., their human-oriented epistemology.

In most cases, then, if religious disagreement is to take place, it cannot do so across these category lines lest it degenerate into covert philosophical debate. Traditionalists of one religion must engage traditionalists of another religion (though, as noted above, if they are absolutists, it is difficult to see how they can speak to one another as equals). Liberals must argue with liberals. Only then do the genuine religious divisions emerge and confront each other. For traditionalist Jews to cite liberal Christian disbelief as evidence against the beliefs of Christian traditionalists is, therefore, inappropriate. Jewish traditionalists would utterly reject the same liberal standards of judgment as applied to Judaism, e.g., that a future resurrection is unbelievable because it violates our scientific view of reality. I have pointed above to the problems of the liberal Jewish criticism of traditionalist Christianity and more on this theme will be said in Chapter VI, "The Christ and Ethics."

I have taken the possibility of engaging traditionalist christologies about as far as I usefully can. I shall want to devote a separate chapter to liberal christologies since I can engage them in some depth from a liberal Jewish viewpoint. Because I believe an additional theological category exists today, that of the post-liberals, I shall then move on to discuss what I would call post-liberal christologies from a similar Jewish perspective. For substantive reasons the relation of the Christ to ethics and to culture will each be treated in a separate chapter.

There is an additional logical possibility that it seems appropriate to consider here: that religious differences might be evaluated by a universal standard of truth. Three contemporary candidates for so exalted a role deserve consideration: philosophy, sociology and comparative religion.

As a current exponent of the philosophic option let us consider a suggestion by Charles Davis to departicularize theology into the study of religion generally (1974, pp. 207–208). This would begin by an effort "to lay bare the grounds of human consciousness in its structure and contents" (p. 210). For Davis theology cannot any longer have a dogmatic foundation but must grow out of the very nature of thinking and being. Davis explicitly understands this to mean the sort of insight gained via the critical philosophy of Kant and Heidegger. Christian faith needs to validate itself in terms of their universal structuring of human thought (p. 211). This will finally resolve the institutional problems created by teaching particular religions at a university, for all academic activity there presumes a community of truth and a high degree of openness to others' ideas.

Three responses were given to Davis's statement. William Hordern seems largely to agree with Davis for he tries only to define who should and who should not properly teach in a religious studies program (p. 234). Kenneth Hamilton, however, points out that in Davis's argument methodology has gone on to make "metaphysical" claims. That is, assumptions that are useful for playing the "religious-studies-game" are taken as saying something about reality itself and become prescriptive about what constitutes true religion. William Fennell gives this a fuller philosophical exposition. He charges Davis with not demonstrating the validity of his universalist standards (pp. 222ff).

I think this latter point worthy of brief extension. Every argument made for the relativity of religion as demonstrated by its inner changes through history or its contemporary pluralism may as effectively be applied to philosophy as to religion. The possibility that a move from a Liebnizian universe to that of Russell or Quine might also occur to Kant and Heidegger in the immediate future often makes modern philosophers humble about their claims, including those they make against religion. However, they are less likely, in my experience, to recognize that the very notion of a "universal ground of human thought" is under radical challenge because philosophy today is highly pluralistic. Philosophers calling for a universal frame for thinking rarely face up to the irremediable conflicting methodogical claims of other philosophers. Worse, when they seek to think universally, they generally exclude from consideration any non-Western, non-university-level thought patterns, a guild-consciousness they would find intolerable in theologians or religionists. How deep this challenge might go was set forth by the Japanese philosopher Masao Abe who inquired why Western thinkers always took the givenness of being as the basis of their thought when Asian philosophers often took the reality of nonbeing as their starting point (1975, pp. 181–192). Frederick Sontag's reply gives a good indication of how culture-bound our sense of universalism is (1975, pp. 421–431).

Critical philosophy has taught us to be critical to the claims of philosophy itself. The claim that one or another thinker, e.g., Kant or Heidegger, has given us such a universal sense of truth that religion must adapt itself to it, seems grandiose in view of the shifts that can occur in the philosophic consensus—or its breakdown. Philosophy's claim to preeminence over religion is no longer self-evidently true. Anyone hoping to validate such a hierarchy must first demonstrate the existence of a universally accepted metaphysics or its equivalent, a most unlikely possibility in our pluralistic time.

A prototypical Jewish experience in this vein is Hermann Cohen's effort to validate a universal, neo-Kantian "religion of reason" and then reinterpret Judaism in terms of it. For some decades Cohen's philosophic reworking of Judaism dominated modern Jewish intellectual life. It does so no longer for several very instructive reasons. Cohen's neo-Kantian definition of "reason" carries little philosophic conviction these days. More importantly, his reading of traditional Judaism, for all its intrinsic interest, reveals more about his philosophical hermeneutic than it does about historical Judaism. And, I do not see that any philosophy today can claim such universal validity that all religions should agree to debate their beliefs in its terms.

A second candidate for a transcendent criterion of religion is sociology. Robert N. Bellah can say, though with more qualification than is reproduced here, ". . . religion is one for the same reason that science is one—though in different ways—because man is one . . . I am not advocating the abandonment of the canons of scientific objectivity or of value neutrality . . . But they do not . . . relieve us of the burden of communicating to our students the meaning and value of religion along with its analysis. If this seems to confuse the role of the theologian and scientist, of teaching religion and teaching about religion, then so be it" (1970, p. 96). A more triumphalist statement of this position appears in William C. Shepherd's "On the Concept of 'Being Wrong' Religiously" (1974, pp. 66–81). Shepherd argues from the premise that sociology shows all religion to be highly integrated into the fundamental ethos of its culture. A religion that is not so situated may therefore be said to be "wrong." Our culture is thoroughly pluralistic. Therefore religions that are exclusivistic or, more positively, which do not have and do not reach out to multiple symbol possibilities for confronting reality, are not right for modern man.

Professor Shepherd not only commits the logical error of converting sociological description into prescription, he ignores the simple data of the history of religion. For all that religions are socially integrated they are also often (if not always) in conflict with their cultures. Surely that has been the experience of Jews in the diaspora for two thousand years, and of Christians in the early days of the Church, and it remains an element of some of the theologies described by Richard Niebuhr in his book *Christ and Culture*. (On this see Chapter VII.) Equally significant is the fact that this issue cannot be argued with Professor Shepherd despite all his putative openness. He identifies all efforts to reinterpret traditional religion as the psychological defensive maneuver called "secondary elaboration," a somewhat less derisive term than "rationalization," though with much the same impact. This precludes his having any discussion with particularists. One cannot engage someone in discussion whose only response is, "Why are you being so defensive?"—unless, of course, one wishes to accept that person as one's psychoanalyst. Thus Shepherd's Norman Brownian, polymorphously perverse, free-swinging, multiple-symboled, change-oriented religion, is advocated with a dogmatism as unconfrontable as Barth's or Berkouwer's. The texts and beliefs diverge; the orthodox stance is the same.

A third possible way of finding a vantage that transcends that of any particular faith arises from the comparative study of religion. A particulary interesting example of this option is given by John Hick in the second edition (1973) of his *Philosophy of Religion* in the newly added chapter "The Conflicting Truth Claims of Different Religions." Since Hick is a philosopher of note and his chapter begins with a consideration of William Christian's *Oppositions of Religious Doctrines*, one might expect Hick to deal with this matter in conceptual terms. Instead he approaches it entirely from a socio-historical perspective. Basing himself largely on Wilfred Cantwell Smith's work, Hick argues that difference in religion is essentially due to cultural provenance. "This means that it is not appropriate to speak of a religion as being true or false . . . For the religions, in the sense of distinguishable religiocultural streams within man's history, are expressions of the diversities of human types and temperaments and thought forms" (p. 124). This "did not come about because religious reality required this, but because such a development was historically inevitable in the days of undeveloped communication between the cultural groups. But now that the world has become a communicational unity, we are moving into a new situation in which it becomes both possible and appropriate for religious thinking to transcend these cultural-historical boundaries" (p. 124).

Hick considers three realms in which divergent truth-claims will have to be met. First, with regard to our diverse modes of experiencing divine reality—of which the personal/impersonal views of God are a key instance—he argues that these are not differences of principle. If we could think in terms of infinite as against finite reality, he believes such disagreements could be transcended (128). As to our differences in doctrine and theory, he holds that these have changed before and are undergoing rapid development today. As faiths meet and interact they are likely to reach intellectual unity (128). The greatest difficulty we face is our divergence over central symbols or revelatory events, in Christianity, the Christ. These need to be subordinated to our universal affirmations, the particularity of christology being reinterpreted in terms of the faith that God's love extends to all humankind. He derides efforts to extend salvation to those outside the Church as "an epicycle of theory, complicating a basically dubious dogmatic system and not going to the heart of the problem" (129). Christian thinkers today have a clear responsibility to find ways to departicularize the Christ.

What surprises one in reading this material is Hick's sudden loss of philosophical acumen (see Lipner, 1976, p. 227). Inferences from history are notoriously treacherous, yet they abound in these pages. Only humility in statement compensates for a lack of self-criticism in assertion. The finding that unity undergirds all human religion is surely not substantiated by the history of religion. All its data show pluralism. To convert these into a unity requires a transempirical principle. Such a principle is not itself empirically or historically derivable. To establish the reality of such an all-embracing unity underlying particularity has defeated the efforts of major philosophers since Hegel. To assert such a thesis now is no trivial matter—yet Hick treats it as if it requires no substantiation. Hick's dismissal of particularity is based on an assumption as comprehensive as it is unproved. Jews, Christians and Moslems, because they believe in a universal God, can assert that one God is the basis for all true religion despite its diverse forms. Their universalism derives from a particularistic base that it could therefore contradict only at its own peril.

While it is true that religions are largely cultural-historical phenomena, this does not require us to say that their particularity is entirely a human creation. How does Hick know that truth is not or cannot be particular, rather than universal? That it cannot grow in a specific cultural form and develop with historical change? This may not be inferred from the fact that many religions make truth-claims, thereby showing most, more likely all of them, are false. Judaism and some Christian theorists have taught that while their faiths are true, other faiths may be true and need not be completely false. To ascribe particularist truth-claims merely to cultural ignorance of other religions seems contradicted by the experience of some religions. Judaism had centuries of intimate exposure to idol worship and Zoroastrianism and considered them false. It had intense involvement with Christianity for two thousand years and with Islam for more than a millennium. It still does not consider conversion to either merely a sociocultural breach rather than a theological defection.

Hick implies that there is a logical connection between "communication" and the dissolution of religious difference. But does acquaintance necessarily lead to giving up one's individual sense of truth for what all people might possibly agree to? Hick apparently realizes that he has not presented a case for his thesis and continually resorts to telltale linguistic usages such as, "it is possible that their future developments may move . . . " (p. 127), "it may be that in time they will be . . ." (p. 128), and "does not seem impossible . . ." (p. 128). These states of possibility cannot be termed intrinsically illogical. Yet without data or argument to support such statements, the outcome might logically as well be, "it is unlikely that," "it may not happen that" and "it does not seem likely." Hick begins by calling his approach a "hypothesis" (pp. 125, 126) and ends by speaking of "the future I have speculatively projected" (p. 128). What begins as history ends as prophecy and purports to be part of philosophy of religion. The progression is not an uncommon one.

Historians of human religion often begin by utilizing the idea of unity behind particularity so they may generalize their findings and often end up asserting their data proves their premise. Hick, being an accomplished philosopher, should know the chasm separating methodological assumptions from metaphysical assertions. I prefer to believe that in this instance Hick's humanity outran his intellectuality and in the conflict between them he preferred building world community to creating logical arguments.

A good antidote to Hick's sentimentality may be found in Philip Sherrard's essay, "The Tradition and the Traditions: the Confrontation of Religious Doctrines" (1974, pp. 407–417). Sherrard carefully examines some fundamental views of Hinduism and Christianity about ultimate reality and finds them to be substantially contradictory. He does not see how such difference of opinion can easily be overcome. (He does not extend his study to our question of how the issues between the faiths might be joined.) Without minimizing the need to create interreligious appreciation, I believe the price of tolerance cannot be set at self-sacrifice. Religion-in-general is a creation of professors. I do not see that it should lead us to avoid our differences with one another and I do not believe that it can take us very far in debating them.

Traditionalist Jews and Christians will deny that any standard extrinsic to their faith can be utilized to stand in judgment over their divergent perceptions of reality. As long as the claims to overarching perspective are only formal, such as descriptive sociology or history or the claims of linguistic usage or the logic of argument, they cause no problems. However, unreflective liberalism awakened traditionalists to the way in which what begins as the utilization of neutral methods soon winds up as dictating substance. It turns out that "value-free" procedures almost always assume a consensus as to what is proper and thus are covertly prescriptive. The sociologist's or religion professor's expertise in describing social functioning confers no authority for making value-judgments. Religious traditionalists, having seen what has happened to recent human claims to universal truth, will indignantly reject secular wisdom's right to judge divine revelation. Liberals will have to judge in each case whether they find themselves spiritually informed by a given humanistic claim or not, and may come to accept some secular guidance in arbitrating religious disagreement. But just where such truth is to be found today is not clear, the question of authority always being the crisis of liberal theology. Post-liberals speak of God's participation in revelation, though in their view the human partner plays a major, perhaps equal role in it. They will likely be sceptical about the possibility that a purely human source of knowledge provides such truth that it can be the criterion of faiths that are as God-given as they are created by people.*

---

* I have not treated the logic of discussions between religionists and nonbelieving humanists. That would require so great an expansion of this book that, for all its interest, I have not allowed myself to undertake it.

IV. Ruether, Soelle and Schoonenberg: Revitalizing the Liberal Christ

Though there are significant differences in the christologies of Rosemary Ruether, Dorothee Soelle and Piet Schoonenberg, most noticeably in the role God plays in them, their approach to the Christ is sufficiently similar that they may usefully be considered as a group. By contrast to the traditionalist theologians, their emphasis on the human aspect of the Christ is so great that their work merits the appellation "liberal."

Only two portions of Rosemary Ruether's unpublished manuscript *Messiah of Israel and Cosmic Christ* are currently available. One of these deals with the social relevance of Christian Messianism and is not directly relevant to our topic (1972b). The other, a section of the book's conclusion, summarizes her work (1972a). It may be taken as a good indication of her thought until the full text is available.

Ruether's stance is clearly not traditionalist. Her reference to the "Messiah of Israel" in the title of her work is not a *pro forma* bow in the direction of "Old Testament" teaching. She takes Jewish Messianism seriously, recognizing that the expectation of Hebrew scriptures has continued unabated in Jewish piety to the present day. More, she gives credence to its implied criticism of Christianity's assertion that Jesus was the Messiah. "Yet, in asking ourselves what it meant two thousand years ago and what it can mean today to say that 'Jesus was the Christ,' the Christian must also reckon with the equally inescapable fact that the mes-

sianic age has not come" (p. 17). Rather than revise the Israelite
sense of Messianic expectation as a result of Jesus' delay in returning—the classic Christian strategy (pp. 17–18)—Ruether believes it is necessary to rethink the Christian interpretation of
Christ-hood. For her, the cosmological christologies were developed as a result of the early Christians' disappointed expectations (p. 18). She sees these doctrines as "less about Jesus than
. . . making Jesus the symbol of all that mankind and creation
'ought to be.' Christology is the myth of transcendent or ideal
anthropology and cosmology" (19).

Her search for a formula to describe the Christ in view of
his not having reappeared begins critically. Ruether rejects all
traditionalist christologies with their assertions of Jesus' uniqueness and once-for-all-time character. She is also unpersuaded by
Wolfhart Pannenberg's historicism. "It is also hard to know how
all human history can again be dovetailed into a process beginning with Jesus, in a literal sense, without a new Christian paro-
chialism that must reject the validity of the religious starting
points of people of other cultures. Christianity again threatens
to become a closed ideological universe in which other people's
paradigmatic events must be discounted as 'false gods' . . . " (p.
21). A similar radical concern for the universal validity of religious experience is found in her identification with Rubem Al-
ves's criticism of Jurgen Moltmann for not considering that the
Bible's transcendent call "might itself be a projection of an exi-
gency universal to human nature" (p. 21). She spurns a theology
of progress, with Christ's kingdom coming gradually, because
such a theory "would make it almost impossible for the Christian to make sense out of the history of non-Christian peoples"
(p. 22).

Positively, Ruether seeks to establish Jesus "as our paradigm of man." He cannot then be seen as "a finalization of an
ideal" but he is "our paradigm of hoping, aspiring man, ventur-
ing his life in expectation of the Kingdom." The term "Christ"
should be understood as "the symbol of the fulfillment of that
hope. Jesus-Christ, then, stands for that unification of man with
his destiny which has still not come, but in whose light we continue to hope and struggle." Through this symbol we gain ac-

cess to "the hoping One" and have a foretaste of the kingdom to come. Because, too, we recognize that the Powers and Principalities of Evil have, in effect, been dethroned, we gain the courage to fight against them in history. Out of the experience of such a life of transcendently powered hope Ruether believes one might honestly now say "Jesus has already been the Christ. Again, this affirmation is paradigmatic for the structure of human existence and not something unique about Jesus. Jesus-is-the-Christ stands as an archetype, for us, of aspiring man who, in reaching for the Kingdom, lays claim to this present earth in such a way that the evil powers are already conquered in principle" (p. 22). As a result of this universalization, the Jew "does not need to know about his faith through the story of Jesus, because he already has other stories that tell him the same thing, such as the story of the Exodus" (p. 23).

Three characteristic signs of the liberal position are clearly seen here. God retreats from the foreground of the religious scene. Though mentioned from time to time, God's role is relatively passive and inactive compared to what is done by humankind. What were once decisive divine acts are translated into human hopes, ideals, experiences or accomplishments. This stems from a horizon of religious truth that includes all humankind. Religious uniqueness is reduced to a social or historical category that, though real, is not normative. Instead the theologian humbly reaches out to all peoples open to the truth they may possess.

These themes also appear in the christology of Dorothee Soelle. The explicit context for her discussion of the Christ is the "death of God" (1967, p. 10). This secularistic framework necessarily results in a christology done "from below." Soelle carries this out by inquiring what might be meant today by "one of the oldest titles of Christ . . . Representative" (p. 13). Her analysis proceeds from contemporary man's need for identity. ". . . the Western tradition cannot break this law it has inherited, that identity always implies irreplaceable and non-exchangeable being" (p. 33). The search for a genuine identity is central to our culture and accordingly she develops her argument for the

Christ in terms of two aspects of individuality, irreplaceability and relationship. "Man cannot be thought of as a self-sufficient being. Identity is not achieved independently" (p. 33). "I am irreplaceable only for those who love me ... for those who set their hope in me" (p. 46).

For Soelle, relationship necessarily implies representation. When one represents someone, that person must be irreplaceable. By contrast, when one substitutes for somebody the original person is dispensed with. As a result, where there is genuine representation, that is, representation without the desire to be a substitute, then the represented one is assured of irreplaceable individuality and, hence, identity (pp. 20ff). That does not lead Soelle to posit Christ as our-representative-in-fact, as a consequence of whose action we can claim genuine identity. In a secular time such as ours, this would be seen as a metaphysical assertion about the Christ and his work, and it would be dismissed as mythological. Pursuant to her stated goals Soelle does not yet make any claims for what God has done in Christ or speculate about what one might personally know after the experience of having been properly represented. Rather she begins with the human situation and seeks to demonstrate our need of representation. Once it has been established that people must be represented if they are to have a genuine identity, then they will be ready to see what the Christ might mean to them.

Soelle's argument proceeds on two levels, that of personality and that of temporality. Personality inevitably means dependency. "All this presupposes that man is a being who needs representation. This dependence on representation cannot be dismissed as a relapse into immaturity nor be regarded as an unenlightened mythological archaism. The conception of man as a self-sufficient hero, needing no-one's help, relying on himself ... is confronted by the other conception of man—man unable, today, to take responsibility for himself; aware of not being self-contained ... " (pp. 46–47). "By accepting himself in his weakness and dependence, he continues, consciously or unconsciously, his search for a representative" (p. 51). "Because personal being—except in conflict—means dependent being,

man needs to be represented" (p. 53). Neither what other individuals or society as a whole does to represent us is adequate to
our needs (p. 54).

One must also think of man's "dependent being as radical
expression of his being-in-time. . . . [I]n the search for personal
identity, time is . . . the hope of those who lack identity. If I am
irreplaceable but can be represented, I have gained time. . . .
Where I am irreplaceable, I must be represented; because I am
irreplaceable, I must be represented. . . . We have, with that, defined the conditions under which representation can appear:
personality and temporality" (p. 55). Perhaps the temporality
argument is more clearly put later. "The very fact that a man's
life is not completely contained in his present success or failure,
but always includes an element that is still future, means that he
needs representation" (p. 102).

Once this understanding of the human condition has been
set forth, Soelle can move on to explain that Jesus sought to represent all humankind before God but not to be its substitute (p.
103). "He who in our place believes, hopes and loves—and who
therefore does what we failed to do—does not obliterate us so
nothing now depends on us" (p. 103). "By his [the Spirit's] representation, he holds their place open for them lest they should
lose it. Expressing it metaphorically, we need Christ so that God
should not 'sack' us. Without Christ, God would dismiss us on
the spot" (p. 104). This work of representation is not yet complete. Soelle, like Ruether, is sensitive to the issue of Christian
anti-Semitism and sees it as one sign that Christ does not yet
"perfectly and completely secure(s) for us the reconciling grace
of God" (p. 109). Furthermore, the nonsubstitutive, hence provisional representation Soelle outlines should make Christians
humble as to the truth they possess. For her that would make
persecution of others impossible. She also believes her christology enables Christians to appreciate the Jewish insistence that
the redemption has not yet arrived. "Christ enables non-Jews to
become Jews; that is to say, he enables them to live in postpone-
ment" (p. 111).

Soelle does not argue for the Christ as one who had a
unique consciousness of God for this seems to her too perfec-

tionist a model for our troubled time (p. 113). Rather her Christ
is the ideal teacher who shows "readiness to accept without limit, without conditions." He is not merely "a person of exemplary
moral character who conveyed to others various kinds of information" (p. 115). "Christ is the eternal teacher whose work is
never done . . . who in our interests secures us time and delay"
(p. 116). And Christ, like every good teacher, feels the necessary
punishments as much as the student (pp. 119–120). Indeed,
though he depends on our assent, lest he become our replace-
ment, his representation of us is by means of identification with
us in regard to our sin (pp. 123–125). Soelle consistently emphasizes the theology of the cross. All she can say of the resurrection is that it is "the achieved identity of all men." Its
historicity is skirted in the phrase "what his disciples experienced as his resurrection." It is a "symbol" whose meaning derives from the cross (p. 126).

There is a dialectical element to the Christ's work. He represents God to the world for he identified himself not only with
all humankind but with God—and precisely as a provisional
nonsubstitute (p. 134). "This does not only happen where men
speak of God and Christ, where Christ is made explicit" (p.
134). Christ runs ahead "to man—before God has reached them
but in order that he may reach them. There is in the world an
anonymous Christianity, ignorant that it is Christian . . . yet serving his cause" (p. 135). To the objection that the term Christ has
here become "a mere cipher or metaphor" Soelle responds that
until the world understands it by acting on it "the name 'Christ'
is an unbreakable cipher, an 'absolute metaphor' " (p. 136). Jesus lives "as the consciousness of those who represent God and
claim him for each other . . . [Here] the implicit Christ is present" (p. 137).

Now, at the time of the death of God, we see that "God
needs actors to play his part . . . [This] role without him [the
Christ] would remain unfilled" (p. 140). Christ's life thus also
keeps God's place open for him, showing the reality of God's
kingdom while revealing it to be one which has not yet been established on earth (p. 148).

Soelle's presentation indicates the ambivalence of liberalism to the issue of uniqueness in religious truth. Arguing substantially within the human perspective, liberals are loathe to assert that they have a truth that is true for everyone. They do not see how human beings can make the leap from their finitude to comprehend reality as it is, all in all. They prefer to speak only of the truth as they see it.

In Soelle's case we may observe this humility in the starting point she takes for her study. She begins with two givens: the Christian faith in the Christ and a world in which God is dead. She sees her task as reinterpreting the accepted faith in terms that will be meaningful in a dramatically antithetical cultural situation. At this initial stage of the discussion no claims are made as to why the Christ is needed or desirable. That Christianity centers on the Christ is merely a fact. Hence one may avoid the question of the claims the Christ makes on non-Christians and proceed with the question of how Christians ought to talk about him. I take it this is Soelle's way of avoiding the classic difficulty of liberal theologies, how to justify particularist assertions. In Soelle's acceptance of the secular condition of our culture this problem of religious specifics becomes particularly pressing. If God is dead why bother talking about the Christ at all? One might reasonably contend that even as God is dead despite the many churchgoers, so Christianity is dead despite the many people who speak of Jesus the Christ. The issue of the continued relevance of old symbols or communities, Jewish or Christian, plagued the so-called radical theology from its beginning. Its inability to create a persuasive theory of religious particularity in a time of rising ethnic interest was one of the major factors contributing to its youthful senescence.* Soelle skirts this issue by situating herself within a given faith-community and by that existential equivalent of asserting a dogma, proceeds to the question of reinterpretation.

Like many a liberal, she had a hidden agenda. She believes her revealing symbol, the Christ, speaks to a need all human beings have. She is at pains to show everyone must have a repre-

---

* For a recent, sad example, see William Hamilton's defense of his choice of Jesus as a focus for his theology (1974, p. 17).

sentative. Then she seeks to show that Christ is the sought representative and ends with claims for his uniqueness. Thus, as the argument progresses, she can say, "To ask about the structures of living representation is necessarily to ask about Christ" (p. 103). In view of her concern for humanity and its moral autonomy her claims for his lordship are limited. Yet she can describe his status as "an ultimate and final provisionality" (p. 107). Or later in the book, when God-language is resurrected, she can say "Christ produced a new kind of existence in the world" (p. 133). He is "an unbreakable cipher, an 'absolute metaphor' " (p. 137). "God's leading player is Christ . . . [This] role without him would remain unfilled" (p. 140).

What is not clear from this shift in tone is whether the original framework of the argument has been abandoned. If Soelle is being descriptive and only saying "this is the way Christians see things," then the discussion can proceed on the phenomenological level. Sometimes, this is all she claims. "The Christian faith answers all these questions by saying that from now on, representation is . . . the really decisive event of all human history. Anthropology and christology . . . exist in correlation" (p. 103).† Yet not only do the qualifying phrases fall away in the latter pages, the mood rises to one of proclamation. There she moves, far beyond a depiction of the Christ prepared for people whose ability to perceive his significance has been impaired by living in an antitheistic culture. Soelle is speaking to the world, particularly to the unconverted and, despite her careful attention to the Jewish argument about the unredeemed state of the world (pp. 107ff), I cannot tell whether her "invitation to a dialogue" does not move beyond phenomenology to mission.

These are slim grounds on which to hold open the possibility that liberals need not always be the sort of universalists we found Ruether to be. She was eloquent about the spiritual adequacy of other faiths than Christianity, explicitly saying the Jews did not need the Christ since they have the Exodus story. In the absence of any such clear-cut statement by Soelle, the possibility

---

† In her text this statement precedes the citation from p. 103 given in the previous paragraph, thus adding to the evidence for the phenomenological stance.

must be held open that despite the christology from below, she believes everyone ought to accept the Christ. If this is so, she has invited us to more than a phenomenological exchange.

My general doubts about the value of labeling theologies were increased by the ambivalence I felt in classifying Piet Schoonenberg with the liberals. I did so because the central drive and the distinctive approach of his christology is the human-ness of Christ. Since the Church, with Chalcedon, has always insisted on the full humanity of the Christ—"true man"— Schoonenberg, arguing on the basis of what we today understand personhood to be, reinterprets the older doctrines of the Christ (1971, pp. 66ff). Thus he can describe his theory as a "christology of the human final completion" (p. 98).* He can also say that he has reversed the traditional mode of interpreting the Chalcedonian four negatives of the identity-in-separation of Jesus' personhood and Godhood. Instead of his humanity being understood, as it were, in terms of his divinity as the Christ, Schoonenberg sees his Godhood, so to speak, within the framework of his personhood. "Now not the human but the divine nature in Christ is anhypostatic . . ." (p. 87).

This substantial humanization of the Christ is paralleled by a de-emphasis on, and substantive diminution of, the transcendence of God. It is highly significant that Schoonenberg precedes his study on the Christ by another, written originally for a different purpose (p. 7), which analyzes the relation of God to creation, and specifically to people. That essay proceeds from the typical liberal faith that God cannot act in nature in the way described in the Bible. From a scientific perspective, such divine actions are mythical imaginings that cannot be accepted by anyone who sees nature as a closed system of cause and effect. Similarly, to assert that God does not coerce people or preempt their right to act with consequence safeguards humanity's sense of responsibility and its dignity. A new sort of theology is needed to speak to this perception of reality.

Schoonenberg then demonstrates how God's action in the

---

* See the note there as well as his argument on p. 99 against Soelle for making too restricted a claim for Christ's humanity.

world might be understood in a more immanentist fashion than that of traditional Catholicism. All his later discussion of God coming into history is put in these terms. Thus, God's being one with Jesus and the divine participation in Jesus' career, is explained in terms of God's dynamic immanence in nature. Schoonenberg envisions God as the ordering power in nature who leads it to its proper fulfillment. "God realizes nature according to its own course and laws, but he does not intervene in it, he does not intercede, he does not take over the work of a worldly cause, he supersedes nothing, he eliminates nothing . . . [H]e leads the world for us to the best advantage" (p. 25). Schoonenberg often sounds like a process theologian, but he manifests almost no interest in the metaphysical ground of nature which is so strong a feature of that position. Instead I often had the sense that, in a not uncommon liberal fashion, his God was, in effect, the natural order, somewhat optimistically perceived. With Christ-hood reinterpreted in terms of personhood and the supernatural transformed into immanentism, Schoonenberg seemed to me best considered with the other liberal theologians.

Several things trouble me about my classification. Schoonenberg identifies himself as a loyal son of the Roman Catholic Church, and the sort of liberalism I hear in his language accords poorly with some of its official teachings. Moreover, Schoonenberg is at pains to dissociate himself from humanistic liberalism (p. 91) and recognizes the dangers of losing the transcendence of God by an emphasis on immanence (p. 27). He insists that he retains a very real, though reinterpreted sense of transcendence. He further argues that in his doctrine of the two natures in Christ, the distinction between the transcendent and the historical natures is greater than in traditional formulations (p. 92). So too, though Schoonenberg recognizes his affinity to process theology (p. 85, note 16, section b), he also asserts his differences with it. He finds that position inadequate to render the central affirmations of Christianity, specifically the Trinity (p. 86, note 16, section c), the resurrection and continued life of Christ (p. 166, note 68). In the latter case, he speaks for the Bible and God's prerogatives in terms most uncommon among liberals. "I

know all the difficulties of speaking about this absolute and ultimate future, but an *exclusion* of such a future for human subjects
seems to me to detract from 'the scriptures and the power of
God' (Mark 12.24)" (p. 166). Finally, I sense that Schoonenberg
takes for granted a context that is critical to his meaning but
which I do not share. I surmise from the strong emotional un-
dertone of the first essay that he intends his work to be a correc-
tive or counterbalance to what he sees as a one-sided emphasis
in Church teaching. He does not give his readers the full dialectic of his thought but puts his strength on the side he feels needs
stressing.

My intuition in this regard derives from trying to explain
the universalist Jewish philosophies of Hermann Cohen and Leo
Baeck. Against our present situation they could take the Jewishness of their readers for granted and therefore they are almost
exclusively concerned with a Jew's universal responsibilities. So
too, Martin Buber, convinced that role and rule and institution
are the dominant realities in modern existence, plays down his
high estimate of the need and value of law and structure, so he
can concentrate on what he sees us most lacking, a life of interpersonal openness. In their cases, not divining what they take
for granted gives one a distorted view of their teaching. I feel
something of this sort is true of Schoonenberg's christology.

These qualifications to Schoonenberg's liberalism are put
under a shadow by some of his language. As in Soelle's book, we
come across statements where, instead of speaking of his belief,
Schoonenberg suddenly vanishes behind an objective descriptive of tradition. So, his Christ "will be less 'mythical' or 'religious' and more human. Certainly Christ may not be confessed
as less divine than the Church has confessed him, especially in
Chalcedon" (p. 65).† That such a significant qualification is not
directly followed up is to my mind significant. He can also say, in
almost humanistic terms, that because Jesus was "the holy one
of love . . . the New Testament saw the fulfillment of the ideal
figure of Yahweh's servant in Jesus . . ." (p. 96). His treatment of

---

† The succeeding discussion treats of liberals being unable to find themselves in
the Christ.

the resurrection is similarly equivocal. While the resurrection is central to Christian faith, it is not a historical matter but one accessible only to faith (p. 155). A most unexpected passage then follows suggesting that a "sadducaic" interpretation, which denies the possibility of an afterlife, should also be considered, that is "a remembrance of the Lord's death much more than (to) a presence of his person" (p. 159). This statement should be understood in terms of a previous suggestion of the virtue of seeing the resurrection "as a free interpretation of the fact that Jesus' influence somehow pervades." Such a view has the advantages of "doing justice to the Old Testament and thus also of entering into dialogue with modern Judaism" (p. 158). All this culminates in a statement that lunges forward from "can be" to "must and indeed may." ". . . 'Easter' is an event not only in the disciples but also in Jesus. This event can be real without being reducible to the product of the immanent content of our faith. The resurrected Lord can be present as person both for the first witness and for us, without being merely evoked by our memory. On the contrary, he can be primarily the one who calls us and brings us to belief. This is not only possible; we must and indeed may confess that it *is* so, that Jesus Christ thus lives in his completion and in us. This is testified by the first preaching and the whole New Testament, it is repeated by tradition, it is even now still the gospel on which we stand (1 Cor. 15.1)" (p. 160).

Let me now summarize Schoonenberg's concept of Jesus' Christhood. "God fulfills this man in all his dimensions" (p. 193). Jesus is "a holy man, one made holy by God's truth and trust, the one who sanctifies himself for others . . . in a word, the holy one of love" (p. 96). He is not either in essence or accident different from us, yet he is "an absolute culmination . . . eschatological sublimation" (p. 97), "the human final completion" (p. 98). ". . . [T]he fullness of God . . . dwells completely in this Man, but so 'bodily' that it grows with him" (p. 122). Between us and him "The only difference . . . is that the immediacy of his contact with God is predominant . . . [and in this] all his human transcendence lies" (p. 127). The Christ's uniqueness can now be asserted. While all transcendence is prepared for in the structure of human existence, God's call comes "In a totally unique way . . . for Jesus Christ" (p. 44). "Jesus is God's ultimate and complete word . . . in a way which surpasses all God's previous salvific actions" (p. 87 and often).

This has specific consequences for the Jews. "All the believers from this 'first testament' can be described as those who did not achieve perfection, at least not without us and without Christ . . . for we see in Christ the perfection and find in him the foundation, neither of which were yet present for the believers of the Old Testament" (p. 151). "The witness of faith in the Old Testament could not achieve the completion which they looked forward to in their own day; they can only do so now, with us, because Jesus was the first to achieve this completion" (p. 152). The different form of these two assertions is worthy of attention. The former makes a claim for the Christ based only on a given perception, "we see." The latter statement is made in flatly indicative tones. One cannot be certain that the previous perceptual qualification still applies to what is being said. Schoonenberg is that ambiguous.

Jewish liberals can approach Christian liberals with similar grounds of judgment and thus should be able to discuss the Christ. Both begin from human experience, including a high appreciation of what science, social as well as natural, has taught us. Both are sensitive to the many varieties of religious experience. That does not mean that liberals can easily debate religious differences. In some cases there may not be any for, at least from Ruether's point of view, there is no substantial distinction between the truth the Christian has in the Christ and what the Jew possesses in the Exodus stories. They might, however, examine whether this intuition that their faith and its symbols are equivalent is reliable. From a Jewish standpoint there is something troubling about centering one's life around a personal paradigm, in this instance, Jesus the Christ. The equivalent Jewish teaching is the Covenant at Sinai made between God and the people of Israel. The difference is significant. To a Jew, no historic personage is worthy of the status accorded Jesus, particularly when God is immediately accessible and the Torah tradition is in our hands. Jesus as paradigm would seem too easily to lead on to individualism. Centering one's life around the Jewish people's religious experience gives individual existence what Jews believe is a more appropriate social context. With sympathetic Christian liberals such as Ruether, Jewish liberals might then usefully explore the ways in which different religious models entail different consequences; how these affect human life, personal and communal; and how each group seeks to compensate for what seems to the other group the underemphasis that derives from its choice of central symbol.

Both groups of liberals share certain religious problems that derive from their nonexclusivist outlook. They have a similar difficulty giving their particular traditions much authority since their religions can no longer claim unique worth. Liberal Jews must struggle with chosenness in ways somewhat analogous to problems liberal Christians have with the classic doctrine of the Christ. The two faiths can then profitably discuss how to deal with the symbols of uniqueness in a faith whose truth is understood to be essentially universal; or how much reinterpretation they find a symbol can receive and still retain its authenticity; or why they choose to maintain a separate community and the burdens of a special training if there are no fundamental differences between their faith and that of others.* These would, of course, be largely discussions of spiritual unity rather than of radical religious disagreement. It should nonetheless be interesting to see how the different symbols and self-understandings of the faiths change their perceptions of these mutual problems and the possibilities of solving them.

The extent of the possible agreement between some Christian and Jewish liberals should not be underestimated. Were it not for ethnic or other social factors, there would be little to separate many universalizing Jewish liberals from their Christian counterparts. Some years ago this made Unitarianism or Ethical Culture quite attractive to Jews, particularly to those who found ethics and humanitarianism the most congenial substitute for their ethnic-religious heritage. A similar phenomenon is seen on the Christian side in the static or declining membership of the

---

* For a contemporary Jewish effort to explore this latter problem, see Borowitz (1971, 1975, 1978).

sophisticated Protestant denominations and in the erosion of
loyalty to the Roman Catholic Church which stems from the discovery of what Christians share with all humanity.

The assertion by Christian liberals that their faith, while humanly accessible, is the "completion," "fulfillment" or "climax"
of the human religious search, radically changes the discussion.
Now a Christian claim is made upon others and a common basis
exists for evaluating it, namely, our human experience. A discussion resulting from these premises would finally be dialogue
about differences. While Ruether does not reach this level, it
may be that Soelle does, though, as indicated, I am not certain
that this is the case. For the sake of argument, however, let us
assume she was not presenting merely a descriptive statement
but what William H. Christian calls an "implicit" claim on the
other (1972, p. 19).

Soelle's "claim," then, is that the search for identity shows
the need for representation and it is fulfilled uniquely in the
Christ. Since Jews share the human condition which is the basis
for Soelle's christology, a debate over it can ensue. I suggest the
Jewish contribution to the discussion would begin with an agreement as to the human situation in our time. It may well be described in terms of the need for certainty about one's
irreplaceability. This cannot be a purely personal project for our
individuality is itself partially a social matter. As Buber put it,
one becomes a person only in relationship.

The Jewish disagreement with Soelle arises from her argument for representation. I see three possible forms this argument might take. First, representation is one way, among others,
that an individual might know irreplaceability. This is a purely
general assertion that does not entail any special claims for the
Christ. It thus does not provide a basis for discussing the differences between Judaism and Christianity. Second, Soelle might
be arguing that humanity has already been represented in the
work of the Christ, hence individuality and identity are now assured. This is not the way her thought is framed for she wished
to begin with secular human experience and create a christology
from below. In an argument beginning with Christ's representation as fact, one begins, in effect, from above, exposing oneself

to the charge of mythology. To avoid such a dogmatic premise, one might say the fact of our representation by the Christ is an accepted basis of Christian faith. Localizing the thesis saves it from debate, but at the cost of retreating to description and the phenomenological level of discussion. Hence the third possibility, which fits much of Soelle's presentation, seems the only one that will allow for the serious confrontation of religious differences, namely that human nature must have representation if it is to find fulfillment.

Most Jewish thinkers, I believe, would deny this. There is, to Jewish sensibility, something peculiarly indirect about such highly personal fulfillment. A representative is a stand-in. If I had a stand-in, I would know I am so precious my place is held and I cannot be substituted for. But is having a stand-in the only or the best way I can find my irreplaceability? Soelle herself can use terms that seem to open other possibilities. "I am irreplaceable only for those who love me . . . I am irreplaceable for those who set their hope in me" (1967, p. 46). Precisely. I need to be loved. In being loved, I know I am irreplaceable; I am individually, personally affirmed. And quite directly for it is I, and no stand-in for me who is loved. I would indeed be dissatisfied if only through my stand-in's being loved were I loved. Jewish liberals would have no difficulty finding human irreplaceability and thus genuine identity through the experience of secular love. They would see no need for a Christ to help them in this regard. They might perhaps extend this to include the Jewish people's intense communal concern for each Jew as seen in its life-style and death practices. That response would be appropriate for the humanistic plane of the early pages of Soelle's book. In its latter section, she shifts the level of discussion to permit a christological resolution of the problem raised by living in a time when personal identity is uncertain (pp. 99ff). Jewish thinkers would deny that one needs a Christ for such assurance of individual worth. They would point to God's Covenant relationship with the people of Israel and thus with each of its members as providing us with an intimate sense of our personal value and irreplaceability. Living day by day in Covenant with God suffuses one's life with a consciousness of God's concern and care (in

whatever way one's liberal theology defines these terms). Something similar could be said about the situation of non-Jews, for
Jewish theology affirms the continuing efficacy of the Covenant
with the children of Noah. Christians may need a representative
to be certain of their individuality; Jews daily awake and, in the
words of the prayerbook, praise God "who has graciously restored my soul. Great is your faithfulness."

From the Jewish view it seems Soelle has turned the possibility of fulfillment through a mediator into an argument for its
necessity. A representative might be a way of establishing my
identity. That does not mean that without being represented a
person cannot achieve a genuine sense of identity. Likewise the
argument for Jesus as teacher *par excellence* says more to us about
Soelle's faith than it does about an ideal teacher-student relationship. Surely the teacher's giving of self (p. 116) is qualitatively different from Jesus' giving his life for others, even as his
vicariously assuming the punishment due all humankind (p.
119) is far removed from a teacher's empathy with a student's
punishment. But these are arguable matters for we are talking
about a human situation we both share. We might then go on to
debate which religious teaching best meets the needs of human
fulfillment (if that remains our major criterion) since there is
substantial difference between the way in which Christianity and
Judaism propose to bring us to it. We could gain a good deal of
insight, I think, from learning how another faith meets the human situation. This would throw the particular emphasis of our
own faith into sharp relief, a sort of modern version of definition
by negation.

We would have a different sort of engagement of differences had Soelle constructed her theology in terms of the Christ
as the ultimate symbol of the reconciliation of humanity with
God. Speaking of him as a "cipher" or a "metaphor" makes possible a christology that emphasizes the limited interpretability of
the Christ. A symbol discloses a reality that far transcends it. It
performs this service through its concreteness and accessibility,
thereby also obscuring some of the far-off truth that it has
opened to us. A liberal christology might then be created by un-

packing the meanings of the Christ-symbol, acknowledging in advance that the picture then gained would be partial and that much of the truth contained in the symbol remained unexplicated.

Let me explore this theological possibility and its consequences for a discussion of differences. Many theologians confess their humility before the awesome topics with which they deal. Instead of this sense of limits being a brief qualification of their work, it can become a major premise of their theology, and they work not at forming coherent rational structures but at such elucidation of religious symbols as they can manage. Their thought is less like classic philosophy than a species of literary or artistic analysis. Such theologians expose aspect after aspect of the meaning of a symbol, emphasizing its exuberant variegation rather than its rational coherence. Since the whole truth could never be fully explicated, we might well be satisfied with the partial truths we had been given because of the illumination they provide. No such doctrine of the Christ appeared in the group of thinkers I read nor do I know of any such approach to a central Jewish theme, for example, the Covenant. Nonetheless, we see something of this approach in contemporary Christian theology, most obviously in the interest in story-theology, and it makes possible another variety of liberal interreligious debate.

Suppose a theologian were to say that while many symbols are possible for the truth, a given one, say the cross or the Torah, is its most adequate or least inadequate representation. The engagement of differences would now have to proceed in a somewhat tentative and delicate way. While there could be some argument over the explicated content of the contrasted symbols, there would always remain the question of its relation to what remained unexplicated, for the symbol functions as a whole and is far greater than any of its levels of interpretation. Insofar as one could communicate some of the significant meanings of the symbol there could be a confrontation of views. Where straightforward exposition had to leave off it might be possible to communicate more of the symbol's message by inviting the outsider to see how the symbol functions in the religious life of the community. Perhaps then it would be feasible, if only allusively, to discuss the relative values believers ascribe to their symbols and to those of others.

This digression already indicates that liberal theologians share a reasonably common concept of religious symbols. They find the notion of symbolism highly useful. It 'points to a peculiarity of religious language, which seeks to speak of a realm for which they have no denotative reference, yet about which they wish to and find they can communicate, albeit with some difficulty. They agree that there are historic, social and emotional concomitants to symbols and without these the symbol loses its power to speak to people. Thus they speak of symbols coming into being and dying and they point out how difficult it is to create a symbol of any richness or to destroy one quickly. They also maintain that there is some cognitive content to significant symbols and these are not merely the accidental result of communal interaction. They believe people can make symbols their own in a very personal way, as in conversion.

What also needs to be pointed out is that this consensus of opinion on symbols is accompanied by a common problematic. Liberal theologians do not know very much about the "logic" of symbols. We do not understand why, other than growing up with them, people choose to use certain symbols; why they prefer them to others; why they give up some symbols; why they remain unmoved by symbols that others in their class or community find deeply meaningful; why, in the same situation, they are deeply taken by a symbol others are indifferent to or offended by. I suggest that if we were able to discuss across religious lines our experience with our symbols, particularly in areas where there was some overlap yet difference—Messiah/Christ—we would gain greater insight into what is involved in religious symbolism. A somewhat similar case could be made for a joint examination of our common theological symbolism, the terms like paradigm, model and myth, which we use to do our work and which also suffer, in various degrees, from the problem of concealing as they reveal.

This problem of mixed levels of communication is encountered as one moves from the rational to the symbolic plane of discussion and is exacerbated if one tries to go on beyond it to the illumination provided by faith. This is the challenge set by Schoonenberg's christology. He first expended great effort to show that God's action in nature is not interventionist and that Jesus' divinity does not make him qualitatively but only quantitatively different from us. Schoonenberg then flatly declares that this perception is available only to a believer. "That God comes to us in human ways does not mean that his presence and the bearers of his presence are no less mysterious . . . Christ's human transcendence is not provable in an objectifiable way, nor even demonstrable . . . [It] is not clear from any of the miracle narratives in the gospel, although for someone who is open to Jesus' person he is the greatest miracle in all these narratives. That he suffered more than any other man cannot be objectively established. That he is without sin can be accepted only by one who has yielded to the honesty and purity of his person . . . he was not a scholar, not a systematic philosopher, not an inventor, not a politician . . ." (p. 95). The Christ himself is the criterion of his expectation for he fulfills it beyond all anticipation. We must know him in faith to understand who he truly is (p. 96). Thus, despite all the show of liberal rationality, we seem suddenly back in the world of Barth and Berkouwer and all of Schoonenberg's claims for the uniqueness of the Christ are given a sudden infusion of power.

Yet this leaves something substantially out of balance in the totality of Schoonenberg's argument, particularly when we keep in mind his juxtaposing his paper on God's relation to nature with his study on the Christ. On the one hand, Schoonenberg equivocates at God's creation of the world (pp. 19ff); makes God so immanent that he must scramble to explain God's independence of the world (p. 29); insists that "If God gives us his supernatural grace, this can only happen by his directing us to one another as giving men" (p. 41); and in other liberal ways reworks traditional Christian christology (two-natures, preexistence, resurrection). On the other hand, against all the reasonable evidence he can appeal to faith to show us, if we are "open," that Jesus is the unique man-God. Reason had a major role in determining what Schoonenberg could or could not believe in the former cases. Then, when it came to discussing God's total presence in the Christ, he seems able to believe things that are distant if not, at least to Jewish eyes, contrary to reason. Nowhere in these two papers does Schoonenberg clarify the nature of this climactic faith and its relation to the reason he relied on so heavily to set the framework for his thinking. As a result, we cannot tell how to proceed with the discussion. Jews can agree with Schoonenberg that grace "is a covenant relationship" (p. 45) but then the grace Jews know is snatched from them by a faith that sees Israel as having only a "promise" whose "completion in Jesus Christ is purely a gift" (p. 49).

Perhaps Schoonenberg is only following an honored Roman Catholic model. He utilizes philosophy to take the human mind as far as it will go and then allows supernatural grace to fill out the full truth. His reworking of that model makes me unable to follow him. Since he began by virtually eliminating the supernatural realm from which grace might proceed, I do not see where he then draws it from. Or, equally troubling to me, having known all along that supernatural grace operated in contemporary religious lives, why was he at such pains to make God's acts in history utterly immanent? Had he continued with the sort of liberal argument that reinterprets Chalcedon as the achievement of the divine potential implicit in every person, then our common conception of fulfilled humanhood would have allowed Jewish thinkers to discuss why they do not see Jesus of Nazareth as the perfect person. But when the humanism is suddenly banished by an appeal to faith, the possibility of interreligious debate ends and we are returned to the phenomenological level.

Schoonenberg opens up the problem of the discussion of differences when religious discourse proceeds partially on the grounds of reason and partially on the grounds of faith. This moves us beyond liberal theology, whether done by creating rational systems or by explicating symbols. I see in the intermixing of faith and reason a new category of theological discourse, one more reliant on reason than traditionalists have been (perhaps my limited knowledge of Catholicism shows here), yet more traditional in faith than the liberals. This brings us to what I have termed post-liberal christologies.

V. Rahner and Moltmann: The Post-Liberal Christ

In the christologies of Karl Rahner and Jurgen Moltmann a substantial appeal is made to human reason though reason is neither the final criterion of an acceptable christology nor a sufficient basis for Christian faith. Such a mixture of modes of argument creates special opportunities and problems for the confrontation of religious differences, and I have therefore put them in a category of their own so as to give them special consideration.

Having presented Piet Schoonenberg's christology in advance of Karl Rahner's is, inadvertently, likely to diminish the impact of Rahner's achievement. As indicated above, Schoonenberg develops a christology from below in which Christ-hood is the potential of every man. This anthropological possibility is properly fulfilled only in Jesus. Since the God working within all people comes to final and absolute fruition in Jesus, his God-manhood has been given an explanation that does far less violence to modern sensibilities than the substance explanations of Chalcedon do. This recasting of christology from essentialist to existentialist terms was not primarily the accomplishment of Schoonenberg but of Karl Rahner some decades previously. Rahner demonstrated that one could establish an existential base for theological construction and became the great exemplar of christology developed as the logical fulfillment of the universal structure of being human. One indication of Schoonenberg's dependence on Rahner is the fact that the latter is cited more often in Schoonenberg's *The Christ* than any other theologian, including Thomas Aquinas. (Compare the entries, pp. 190 and 189.) Having dealt with this theological approach briefly above, I mention this only in order that my presentation not misrepresent my appreciation of Rahner's extraordinary intellectual accomplishment.

Schoonenberg's distinctive contribution to christology is found in his emphasis on the immanence of God's action. That fits nicely with his other major theme, influenced by Rahner, that humanity's very structure of being is God-oriented and uniquely fulfilled in Jesus. By contrast, Rahner, as we shall see, accompanies his philosophy of being human with a significant emphasis on God's transcendence.

Rahner's thinking has often been associated with that of Martin Heidegger. He differs substantially from the philosophic existentialist in the procedure he uses to elicit the structures of our human situation. Rahner utilizes the transcendental method initiated by Marechal, one which seeks for the a priori of human existence in a way uncongenial to Heidegger's more phenomenological approach. By dint of an analysis of "the unthematic knowledge of Absolute Being given in every objective judgment" (Roberts, 1967, p. 20), Rahner shows that one of the significant existentials of human existence is, in his terms, supernatural. That is, people by their very nature are God-oriented and thus, in turn, "man is a being who is oriented towards a saving event which [it] is possible to expect" (Rahner, 1969, p. 197).

This philosophic groundwork becomes the basis of what I see, for purposes of this study, as the two special contributions of Rahner's christology. The first of these is Rahner's effort to make the doctrine "more intelligible and existentially assimilable" (p. 197). He describes his task this way as he opens his discussion of contemporary christology, "The most urgent task . . . is to formulate the Church's dogma . . . in such a way that the true meaning of these statements can be understood, and all trace of a mythology impossible to accept nowadays is excluded" (p. 196). Rahner's further argument, as to why all people of morally good will should believe in Jesus as the Christ, I would consider his second major theological accomplishment.

With regard to the first theme, there are two ways in which Rahner seeks to make the classic doctrine of the Christ believable today. The one consists of redefining our need to be saved. Rahner demonstrates that people, by the very fact of their being human, implicitly await God's salvation. ". . . man in virtue of his history and his temporal character seeks the ultimate and definitive fulfillment of his existence precisely in history (where the same things do not always happen and what is final can occur), and in the realization that such an ultimate fulfillment cannot take place without involving the abiding mystery of his existence. . . [I]t has nothing incredible about it. For this starting point merely says that God exists, that he freely wills to be man's salvation, in himself, not merely by his finite gifts, and that this definitive and irrevocable gift of himself is made in history and has been accepted in history on man's part" (p. 199). Thus for Rahner, anthropology, properly understood—with God existing and people God-oriented—inevitably points to christology, that is, to the Christ who is God's "definitive and irrevocable gift of himself."

Through a similar humanistic approach, Rahner transforms the old two-nature understanding of Christ as the God-man. It is "inherent in the essence of man himself to *be* this *potentia obedientialis*, at least in the line of a conceivable and hypothetical prolongation of a spiritual being who is essentially and ecstatically oriented towards God" (p. 197). "The man Jesus lives in a unity of will with the Father which totally dominates his whole reality from the start in an obedience from which he derives his whole human reality: he receives himself purely and simply and permanently from the Father. Always and in every dimension of his existence he has given himself over totally to the Father; by this self-dedication he is able, under God, really to do what we cannot do at all; his fundamental attitude and condition (as radical union of being and consciousness) is radically complete origination from God and dedication to God" (p. 200). Thus, the "personal, human reality of Jesus Christ has entered into such a unique God given union with God that it became God's real self-utterance and a radical gift of God to us" (p. 207). Christ's God-manhood is thus as much a statement of his literal continuity of what is true of all people as it is of his distinction from us. Since his divinity-humanity is implicit in each of us, Rahner contends, it cannot be unbelievable to us though it is perfectly lived in him and radically unfulfilled in us.

Rahner presses his existentialist approach a daring step further. He contends that if people resolutely accept their own existence, they are involved in what may be called an "inquiring christology" (p. 194). Rahner then presents three arguments that should lead such a person to see that his existential "inquiry" is nowhere answered as in Jesus Christ. First, "absolute love bestowed radically and unconditionally on a human being" cannot be justified by the beloved since the latter is finite. It might "speculatively and abstractly" be guaranteed by God but the experience "requires a unity of love of God and of the neighbour in which love of the neighbour is in love of God . . . By that very fact, however, it seeks the God-man, him who as man can be loved with the absolute character of love for God . . ." (p. 195). Second, "Death is the one act . . . in which man as a free being disposes of himself in his entirety" yet it is radical powerlessness. To avoid this absurdity, we must posit "that man obscurely expects or affirms the existence of a death . . . in which the dialectic of activity and powerless suffering is reconciled in death." Since such reconciliation requires a reality which can be the unity that transcends this contradiction, the Christ is again pointed to by our very being (p. 195). Third, people have an eschatological hope for a fulfillment that would not destroy their time-bound, finite personal being. This gives us the sense that even now, in time, an irrevocable direction has been given history, one that testifies to the truth of the Christ. Rahner summarizes in these words, "man is on the look-out for the absolute bringer of salvation and affirms, at least implicitly, in every total act of his nature directed by grace to the immediate presence of God as his goal, that he has already come or will come in the future" (p. 195).

To a believing Jew there is much in Rahner's anthropology that would be thoroughly congenial. The notion that humankind is by its very nature oriented to God is a significant philosophic restatement of themes central to Jewish thought as far back as the stories of the creation of Adam and Eve in God's image and that of the Covenant with the children of Noah. Rahner specifically includes a universal sense of messianic anticipation in the existential structure of humanhood. The same is true of all those modern Jewish thinkers who use anthropology as the ground of their theology (so, in their own philosophical styles, Cohen, Baeck, Kaplan, Buber). The notion is not easily to be found in traditional Jewish sources since the emphasis there is on what God rather than people will do to bring redemption. Apparently the centrality of the human, not the substance of the religion, produces this type of theology, a good instance of the virtues of comparing thinkers of a similar methodological approach.

There is common ground for disagreement as well. Two new debatable topics are likely to appear here to a Jewish thinker. Is the event anticipated in the structure of human existentiality a messianic event in the sense that Judaism has envisioned it, or is it a christological event centering about the work of a Christ, a man-God, a person of the Trinity (whether understood in Chalcedonian or Rahnerian description)? Once the abstract anthropological need has been clarified, we may then inquire whether Jesus of Nazareth satisfies the human expectation of a Messiah.

Rahner's argument for the necessity of a God-man event to fulfill our expectations has a negative and a positive aspect. Refuting our natural incredulity that such a thing might happen, Rahner says, "Only someone who forgets that the essence of man . . . is to be unbounded (thus in this sense, to be un-definable) can suppose that it is impossible for there to be a man, who, precisely by being man in the fullest sense (which we never attain), is God's Existence into the world" (1961, p. 184). Positively, Rahner indicates the need for a Christ rather than a mere Messiah in two of his three arguments for christology in *Sacramentum Mundi* (1969). In the argument from the command to love our neighbor absolutely, he says, ". . . recourse to God himself as guarantor and limit of the absolute character of such love would perhaps be possible speculatively and abstractly . . . But the love whose absolute character is experienced . . . involves more than a divine 'guarantee' which remains transcendent to it. It requires a unity of love of God and of the neighbour in which love of the neighbour is love of God, even if only implicitly, and only thereby is fully absolute. By that very fact, however, it seeks the God-man . . ." (pp. 194–195). A similar resolution results from the argument based on the need to accept death. If this "is not to be an acceptance of the absurd . . . [it] implies that man obscurely expects or affirms the existence of a death (whether it has already taken place or is hoped for in the future) in which the dialectic of activity and powerless suffering . . . is reconciled in death. But that is only the case if the dialectic is resolved by being identical with him who is the ultimate ground of its duality. For man does not affirm abstract ideas and norms as the ground of his nature, but a reality which is already, or which will be, present in his own, historical existence" (p. 195). I do not find the third argument in this series, phrased as two sets of contrary questions, more than a case for a nondivine Messiah. Rahner writes, "Or is it the goal of history because history already bears within it the irrevocable promise of the goal . . ." (p. 195). Exodus, Sinai and the concrete experience of revelation we call Hebrew scripture would clearly seem to us such an "irrevocable promise." Perhaps Rahner has in mind here what he explicitly stated in the previous two arguments, that a personal, individual instance of its fufillment is required to make this hope acceptable. He generalizes on this theme elsewhere, "For this religious piety [as contrasted to a religiosity which understands Christ as "Idea"] can only draw its life in fact from the historical Christ (from him and from no one else, from him and not from an Idea!) because man is continually kept in movement by the existential need to possess God concretely, to 'have to' possess him." Without an anthropological derivation and its occurrence "as something really achieved, the historical message concerning Jesus the Son of God is always in danger of being dismissed as a mere piece of mythology" (1961, p. 187).

There would be no argument from the Jewish side that men existentially seek to "possess God concretely." This is the root of idolatry. Judaism fought its explicit forms strenuously in biblical and Rabbinic days. Judaism is still fundamentally opposed to it in all its contemporary, implicit and existential transformations. Rahner does not merely describe this "need," he seems to approve of it. He believes it to be so basic to our nature that it is a major determinant of God's relations with humanity. Thus, Rahner disparages any unmediated experience of God as the basis of our Messianism. He barely admits that it might "perhaps be possible speculatively and abstractly" to dream of redemption without the Christ, as Jews would do (in relation to his first argument) in terms of the Covenant love of God which grounds the duty to love one's neighbor. So, too, with regard to his second argument, he says a personal example is needed. "For man does not affirm abstract ideas and norms as the ground of his nature . . ." This would seem a rejection of the Jewish ground for believing in resurrection: not a Christ, but God's acts and revelations to the Jewish people.

The issue is not merely a theoretical one about humanity and its capacity to love directly an unseeable God—though to Jews who have for millennia worshiped such a God in life-ordering intensity it seems astonishing that others should not see how easy and even sensible a faith this is. By contrast Jews find the idea of a man also being God fraught with difficulty. If Jesus was in some real and not merely verbal sense true God as well as true man, the possibility exists that his acts or words might be invested with God's absolute authority. Christians who have had to live with that consequence of the two-nature doctrine have derided such a one-sided response to the Christ by labeling it Jesusolatry. Sophisticated theologians will go far out of their way to avoid absolutizing Jesus' humanity. Characteristically, none of the theologians studied in this book attempted to prove Jesus' divine stature by citing his acts or his words. They prefer to speak of his consciousness or will or personal relation to God because they do not want to invest finite models with infinite seriousness. Obviously bringing God close to humankind through God's coexistence with man has pedagogic and spiritual advantages. At the same time God's transcendence might be obscured through God's identification with a contingent creature. From the Jewish perspective such a move to immanence is particularly troublesome because it detracts from God's commanding power and our sense that the best of our efforts is less than what God wants of us. The issue is not whether God is easily available to us, for Judaism has its own sense of immanence without any doctrine of incarnation, and my statements here about the importance of transcendence in Judaism should be balanced by my previous discussion of God's nearness, presence and desire for human turning. (As to Jesus as personal model, see below.)

Had Rahner only spoken about all people being created in the image of God and Jesus as exemplifying that image most perfectly we could merely have argued the definition of image and its fulfillment. But Rahner's Jesus is more than God-like, more than the most God-like person who ever lived. He is, while utterly like us, also utterly different from any person who ever has or ever will live. He has so fully realized the Godliness in each person that, he "is" God. By contrast, the finest Jew who ever lived, the one to whom God spoke "as a man to his neighbor," Moses, is a sinner like the rest of us, yet God's beloved. Jews have personal models but see no perfection except in God alone. They have revelation for guidance and a knowledge that they are God-like enough to do God's will or repent for their sins. Compared to God incarnate in Jesus, that is abstract but it surely avoids any semblance of idolatry. Believing Jews consider any human need to "possess" God an impiety that easily can give way to blasphemy. Hence though they await the Messiah they do not understand why humanity in general and Jews in particular require a Christ.

This structural disagreement is matched by one on the level of substance. Again and again Rahner claims that Jesus as the Messiah-Christ is the perfection of the possibilities inherent in humankind. I see this as the existentialist, anthropological substitute for the traditional argument for Jesus' Messiah-ship by his fulfillment of scripture. Rahner specifies that this is to be seen in the perfection of his obedience to God's will, understood in a personal, relational way. I do not see how we can easily determine the quality or direction of Jesus' inner life. The Gospel accounts speak more directly of his words and acts than of his existential stance. Hence the Jewish judgment of his complete fulfillment of the human potential will be directed more to how he lived and died rather than to a second-level interpretation of the will behind the events, though these are closely intertwined.

For the purpose of clarifying the Jewish contrary position it will be useful to focus on an apparent contradiction in Rahner's thought. When it comes to the accessibility of God, Rahner is an enemy of abstraction and generalization and demands concretion. When it comes to Jesus as the perfect person, Rahner is content to discuss this in, what seems to Jewish eyes, his abstract fulfillment of various human capacities. Thus, though Jesus is an exemplar of love, he is not shown to us as having loved any one particular person with the fullness of personal exposure and responsibility that love can entail in the experience of marriage. (Apparently this is something of an embarrassment to some Christians today to the extent that recently a book was published arguing that Jesus must have been married!) Then again, the historicity of Jesus is a critical part of his appeal, but he never became involved in the specific activities in which most people take their greatest single responsibility for the continuity of history, parenthood and child-rearing. He is understood to have identified his life and death with all mankind yet he never participated in the realities of reconciling personal salvation with social and political leadership, which most human beings engage in by undertaking institutional responsibilities. So though Jesus may be a good man, an unusual teacher, a pietist with a strong appeal to many people and great charisma (in the Weberian sense), while one might wish to say that he fulfills a number of significant human potentialities, to say that he is the perfection of the whole of our humanity makes very little sense to Jews. And to say that he does this in so qualitatively unique a way that he is "god's Existence in history," the God-man, person of the Trinity, is incomprehensible to a believing Jew. (I think the same would be true of most of the many Jewish secular humanists with their this-worldly sense of what it is to be a "real person.") As Rahner apparently does not see the adequacy of our "abstractness" about God, so we do not see the attraction of a model far removed from the basic human experiences of most people. I suppose we are involved here in the problem of how specific a symbol needs to be to function properly. Jews prefer to err on the side of being abstract in relation to God and concrete in relation to human duty.

If the issue is returned to the question of obedience to God, we Jews do not think we have much to learn from Jesus. We cannot here discuss the complex issue of the relation of God's will to God's law and of God's law to the Torah commandments and tradition. Let us limit ourselves to what other writers (I did not find this in Rahner) call the critical case, Jesus' obedience to God even unto suffering and death. The accounts are, at the least, humanly impressive and religiously moving. Jews, however, do not consider their own models of obedience inferior in any respect. On the personal level, perhaps the most famous example of obedience is Rabbi Akiba (died ca. 136). The stories of his death—apparently no later from the events involved than those of Jesus' crucifixion—tell of his execution by the Romans. They used iron combs to rake his skin from his body. He seemed so composed, reciting the *Sh'ma* prayer during this process, that his disciples standing nearby asked him about it. He answered that all his life he had pondered the significance of the middle phrase of its verse, "Thou shalt love the Lord thy God with all thy heart, with all thy soul and with all thy might." He had interpreted "with all thy soul" to mean "even if God takes thy soul." The Talmud then reports him as commenting, "I said: when shall I have the opportunity of fulfilling this [commandment]? Now that I have the opportunity shall I not fulfill it? He prolonged the word 'One' until he expired while saying it" (Ber. 61b). To this day, pious Jews, each time they say the *Sh'ma*, "Hear O Israel, the Lord our God, the Lord is one," prolong the word *echad*, "one." To Jews, Akiba seems a more appropriate model than any they know of suffering and dying in personal obedience to God.

However, Jews consider personhood a social as well as an individual matter and therefore the exemplar most adequate to their sense of faithfulness to God is the people of Israel. Not in one life alone, in one day's suffering or in one bitter death has the people of Israel manifested obedience to God. For two millennia a whole folk has been subjected to extraordinary suffering because of their refusal to give up their God. In our time, though the religious motive was replaced by a political one, 6 million Jews were killed because they were Jews. True, many of the Holocaust dead were unbelievers and the inexplicable horror has turned others away from God.* There have always been defectors from the Jewish people and more sinfulness in those who remained than there should have been. That is human nature, hence not surprising. What arouses Jewish awe, the recurrent historical pattern we find numinous, is that in every age, despite every trial, Jews have maintained, revivified and fulfilled their ancient-present Covenant faith. Our era is no different. The survival and devotion of the Jews inspires us beyond anything we know to strive for maximum personal and social obedience to God.

In the ongoing, unfinished, richly meaningful life of the people of Israel, Jews see evidence that God too maintains the Covenant. We do not comprehend much that God does. We do not know why the righteous suffer and the evil thrive. We do not understand why God's face sometimes turns away from us and from humanity. We do not know why the God of life ordains and sometimes hastens death. Yet we know the people of Israel does not survive by its own power alone. God keeps us alive. The uncanny continuity of the Jews is our immediate, renewed and communal experience of resurrection. We regularly fulfill Ezekiel 37, most awesomely now, after Auschwitz. So we trust in God, despite all, and we feel no one offers us more profound or comprehensive symbols for understanding proper obedience to God.

Until now, I have suppressed another part of Rahner's argument. The incarnation is not fully accessible to reason. "... the reality of Christ is intrinsically unique and cannot be derived from anything else ... [I]t is a mystery..." (1961, p. 146).†
Louis Roberts, describing Rahner's method, makes clear that for

---

* The increase of Jewish secularity is one of the few complaints Rahner can bring himself to make about the Jews in his noble response to an inquiry on his attitude toward Jews (1966, pp. 92ff).

† The context here is of special interest for Rahner discusses the uses of reason in dealing with that which transcends it.

Rahner reason and faith interpenetrate (1967, pp. 38ff). In people "The lowest dimension is determined by the highest and the highest by the lowest. Man's supernatural existential penetrates his most physical self." Hence reason unaided gives us no final truth. "Two unique worlds and realities converge, man as the infinite question and the infinite mystery as unlimited, absolute response—and because the mystery still remains, we have that orientation of man and God. So the God-man is the unique and definite answer" (p. 186). Apparently, there is a circle of faith within which one needs to stand in order to see reason through to its fitting conclusions.

This does not end the discussion, for Rahner's notion that philosophy and theology very substantially interpenetrate has a surprising consequence. Rahner believes that knowing the Christ is implicit in all true humanhood. "Anyone who accepts his human reality wholly and without reserve (and it remains uncertain who really does so) has accepted the Son of Man, because in him God accepted man." Thus Rahner speaks of "anonymous Christians" and often writes about them with such power that one has the sense that very many people outside the Church are saved (1969, p. 208; Roberts 1967, pp. 272ff). Then perhaps Jews, despite their ostensible rejection of the Christ do "accept" him when they genuinely understand their human being as grounded in God and pointed toward the coming of the Messiah. I cannot tell how far Rahner's inclusiveness goes or whether he would assign a special status to Jews as a group because of the Covenant or only treat each person in terms of the authenticity of self found there. Rahner is, of course, equally explicit about the uniqueness of the Christ and people's need to accept him wholeheartedly. But enough has been said here to indicate how a discussion of differences might reasonably be carried on between the adherents of a Rahnerian christology and believing Jews.

They might also find it of methodological interest to compare their efforts to explain a traditional, exclusivistic position in terms of modern thought. Rahner's explanation of Christhood may be paralleled by Jewish arguments for the chosenness of the people of Israel. Where Jewish traditionalists speak of

God's sovereign act, which liberals translate into ethnic consciousness or vocation, post-liberals will deal with chosenness in
terms of human spiritual search being met by God's presence
and participation in a special relationship. There are sufficient
similarities in the theological problems involved in explicating a
doctrine of uniqueness that the two sides could learn much from
each other's experience in this regard.

A somewhat altered perspective meets us as we turn to the
work of Jurgen Moltmann. He cites Rahner frequently and, I
judge, more favorably than any other contemporary theologian,
though Moltmann's theory of the Christ is not argued on the basis of a philosophic anthropology. Moltmann uses reason more
dialectically, that is more critically and negatively, than does
Rahner. Correspondingly faith too has a more prominent role in
Moltmann's argument than in Rahner's, yet despite the intensifi-
cation of the two modes of exposition, Moltmann must be classi-
fied with the post-liberals. He attacks traditionalist theologies
like Barth's for their inability to speak to unbelievers except by
preaching. He considers such solipsism too great a price to pay
for theological security, particularly in a world desperately in
need of faith (1974, pp. 66–67). On the other hand the liberals
with their "rosy cross" have been rendered irrelevant by recent
history with its staggering revelations about the human capacity
for evil (pp. 35ff). Moltmann insists that only a theology of the
cross can be adequate to recent human experience and his treatment of the Christ centers on the crucifixion more determinedly
than any other christology dealt with in this book. Of course the
resurrection had dominated his earlier discussion of the Christ
in *Theology of Hope* (1967). By contrast, Moltmann indicates in
the opening pages of his more recent work, *The Crucified God*,
that though he considers the new volume a continuation of his
previous work (1974, pp. 4–5), its altered emphasis derives from
the end of the religio-political movements that seemed so strong
in the 1960's (p. 2). Hope thus must face the realities of human
history, quite specifically the Jewish sense that it is utterly unredeemed (pp. 100ff).

Reason is very much more socially oriented in Moltmann's
thinking than in Rahner's. Moltmann is deeply concerned about

the effects the political and economic orders have upon us. He is highly sensitive to the Marxist demonstration that our social system subverts our personhood and utilizes religion to validate its exploitation of our power. He protests against any Christian theological individualism that permits society to go its way unchallenged. Instead Moltmann insists that religious collusion with dehumanization is un- or even anti-Christian.

This social concern, which dominated his thinking in *Theology of Hope*, is not lessened in *The Crucified God*. But the collapse of the hopes for political change now mandates the shift from a theology of the resurrection to one of the cross. Moltmann notes that even as the previous work was highly influenced by Ernst Bloch, so the newer book is indebted to the critical philosophy of Theodore Adorno and Max Horkheimer. (On the Frankfurt school, see Jay, 1973.) Their thinking represents a continuing critique of society and its operations. They turn a Marxian analysis against Communist as well as capitalist social activities, evaluating the results in terms of a transcendent corporate ideal which, in itself, cannot be directly stated.

Moltmann utilizes this sort of critical analysis to destroy the barrier that society erects between us and the crucified Jesus. Moltmann does not propose to explain away the *skandalon*, the "scandal" of the cross. Rather, he utilizes dialectical reason to show why its affront to our sensibilities is needed if we are to come to God and play our proper role in history. Commonly, we learn by analogy but that process needs to be supplemented by another method, when a thing is known by its opposite. "God only revealed a 'God' in his opposite: godlessness and abandonment by God." This is dialectic, which "does not replace the analogical principle . . . but alone makes it possible" (p. 27). "Without revelation in the opposite, the contradictions [in human experiences?] cannot be brought into correspondence" (p. 28). Moltmann bases his christology on the fundamental paradox of classic Christianity: the Messiah was crucified.

Moltmann uses dialectical reason to clear the way for faith by turning it against simple intellectuality. If the cross "is the point at which *faith* comes into being, this means first of all that Christian theology cannot be a pure theory of God, but must be-

come a critical theory of God . . . polemical, dialectical, antithetical and critical . . ." (p. 69). He insists that "the modern
distinction between fact and interpretation . . . is inappropriate
to the understanding of the 'world of the cross.' This distinction
is essential to modern knowledge, which dominates, which defines in order to affirm and to control what has been affirmed."
In its teaching-preaching Christianity "claims that the crucified
Christ himself speaks and is revealed" (p. 74). He is "more than
the preaching of the cross," yet the message of the crucifixion is
the only adequate access which the godless has to God (p. 75).
For Moltmann, the Christ as person is beyond any particular aspect of his being, even the cross, and he personally remains the
criterion of all judgments to be made of him. As often seen
above this is the common pattern of christologies influenced by
existentialism.

Moltmann's criticism of arguments for faith in Jesus based
on direct moral or metaphysical reasons is, in my non-Christian
estimate, devastating (pp. 97–98). More aptly, Jesus is known as
the Christ "by the future of the kingdom which is inaugurated in
and around him" (p. 98). ". . . the person and history of Jesus
have been manifested and understood as open to the future of
God in the way which was characteristic of the distinctive existence of Israel amongst the nations." Only here "history opens
to the future, and with it messianism has become universal" (p.
99). Thus Christ speaks to the sociopolitical needs of people today who are determined to try to shape the future yet need the
courage and hope to sustain this venture. Faith "is the eschatological anticipation of redemption . . . through one who was an
outcast, rejected and crucified." The crucifixion "makes impossible for a Christian any resigned acceptance of participation in
an unredeemed world" (p. 101). Since Jesus introduces an
unanticipated Messiahship "the novelty represented by Jesus
can no longer be described by recalling anything similar in history or in the future hope, and becomes an open question,
which demands answers which are a confession of faith" (p.
105).

Reason may open the way to one's acquiring faith in the two
great Christian mysteries, the resurrection and the incarnation.

Of the former, it must first be noted that there is no simple continuity or discipleship after his death, as, for example, Socrates had. Thus that Jesus became the one preached by the Church is itself a factor of the resurrection (pp. 122–123). Moltmann then shows how a proper sense of the openness of history is inevitably eschatological. Hence, to have understood Jesus' resurrection as the beginning and validation of the general resurrection to come is to see "the beginning of the end of history in the midst of history" (p. 162). The identity of the resurrected Christ with the historical Jesus is revelatory. It discloses "the eschatological mystery and lies in the faithfulness of God, who manifests himself to be the same . . ." (p. 124). Such speculations about history and eschatology though they "do not 'prove' the justification of the primitive Christian eschatology of the life and death of Jesus . . . do make it more comprehensible" (p. 165).*
This then is connected with Jesus being understood as God-man. "If, as the Easter vision implies, God has identified himself, his judgment and his kingdom with the crucified Jesus, his cross and his helplessness, then conversely the resurrection of the crucified Jesus into the coming glory of God contains within itself the process of the incarnation of the coming God and his glory in the crucified Jesus" (p. 169).

The two-nature theory is thus developed from the theology of the cross. In calling out the famous words of Psalm 22 "Jesus is putting at stake . . . his theological existence, his whole proclamation of God. Thus, ultimately, in his rejection, the deity of his God and the Fatherhood of his Father, which has been brought close to men, are at stake . . . From this point of view, on the cross, not only is Jesus himself in agony, but also the one for whom he lived and spoke, his Father . . . In the death of Jesus the deity of his God and Father is at stake . . . In the theological context of what he preached and lived, the unity of Jesus and God must be emphasized as strongly as this" (pp. 150–151). "The 'Son of God' is . . . the representative and revealer of God in a godless and godforsaken world. That means that God rep-

---

* He utterly rejects Pannenberg's argument for the historicity of the resurrection (pp. 172–173).

resents and reveals himself in the surrender of Jesus and in his passion and death on the cross. But where God represents and reveals himself, he also identifies and defines himself . . . In the action of the Father in delivering up his Son to suffering and to a godless death, God is acting in himself . . ." (p. 192).

Moltmann suggests that to understand the crucifixion properly, one is better off working with Eastern conceptions of the incarnation which are "unrestricted by the doctrine of the two natures by which God and man are distinguished" (p. 206). Rather "the theology of the cross must be the doctrine of the Trinity" and vice versa (p. 241). ". . . the Father delivers up his Son on the cross in order to be the Father of those who are delivered up . . . In the forsakenness of the Son the Father also forsakes himself. In the surrender of the Son the Father also surrenders himself, though not in the same way . . . We cannot therefore say . . . that the Father also suffered and died. The suffering and dying of the Son, forsaken by the Father, is a different kind of suffering from the suffering of the Father in the death of the Son . . . The grief of the Father is here just as important as the death of the Son . . . and if God has constituted himself as the Father of Jesus Christ, then he also suffers the death of this Fatherhood in the death of his Son. Unless this were so, the doctrine of the Trinity would still have a monotheistic background" (p. 243). Moltmann explains the one substance tradition in this way: "God *is* love, that is, he exists in love. He constitutes his existence in the event of his love. He exists as love in the event of the cross. Thus . . . it is possible to talk of a *homoousion*, in respect of an identity of substance, the community of will of the Father and the Son on the cross. However, the unity contains not only identity of substance but also the wholly and utterly different character and inequality of the event on the cross" (p. 244).

Any Jewish response to Moltmann's christology should first acknowledge that, in a way unparalleled by the other theologians studied here, he has learned from contemporary Jewish thought. His argument about the Messianism implicit in an open sense of human history and his social emphasis, empowered by a Marxian analysis, is derived from Bloch, while the critical dialectic is taken from Adorno and Horkheimer, all Jews. In effect, Moltmann provides a religious ground for the demythologized Messianism of these thinkers who, in typical modern Jewish fashion, have secularized the traditional belief into politics or, less courageously, social analysis.† Moltmann also is concerned with Jewish religious thinkers, citing Cohen, Baeck, Buber and Rosenzweig, engaging Ben Chorin and Scholem in a debate on the Christian appreciation of the unredeemed quality of the world, and quoting Heschel's theory of God's pathos at great length. I do not think it too much to say that, whether in response to secular or religious Jewish criticism of Christianity, Moltmann's thought is significantly influenced by what he has learned from personal dialogue with Judaism. Not surprisingly then, there are substantial areas of agreement between Moltmann and contemporary Jewish thinkers. This provides a basis for debating those issues that Moltmann suggests cause Judaism and Christianity to part ways.

A major difference arises from the Jewish charge that Jesus cannot be the promised Messiah for the world remains unredeemed (pp. 100–106). Moltmann is astonished that anyone could think that Christians truly believe that they have already been redeemed. Or that, as against Jewish notions of an exterior, worldly redemption, Christianity teaches a personalist, "interior" redemption (p. 100). He does admit that sometimes Christianity showed an "abandonment of real and universal hope of redemption, and at the same time a cessation of suffering over the unredeemed state of the world" (p. 100). This may be explained as the unfortunate reactions to the disappointments in the expectation of Jesus' early return and the identification of the Church with the kingdom (p. 101). "But is this still authentic Christian faith? . . . [for that] is the eschatological anticipation of redemption . . . through one who was an outcast, rejected and crucified." The crucifixion "makes impossible for a Christian any spiritualization or individualization of salvation,

---

† Jay clearly shows the significance of the Jewish background of the Frankfurt school to which the latter two belonged (1973, pp. 31–37).

and any resigned acceptance of participation in an unredeemed world" (p. 101).

The peculiar logic of these last three statements requires a comment. Taken as an indicative statement the final citation is simply false. The rhetorical question and exposition following it are not a description of historic Christianity or modern Christian thought. Rather the thinker is by this sweeping sort of assertion proclaiming that his personal interpretation of doctrine is the one, correct version of religious truth and all contrary ones are false. This form of discourse is often utilized in Jewish as well as Christian theological writing. It is an accepted device for saying things about a religious tradition which are not (as in the last sentence) or may not be (as in the former two sentences) true about it, but which one feels ought to be true about it and in one's reworking of the tradition are true about it. Jews would find Moltmann's personal interpretation of Christianity close to some of their doctrine. But they would not find his theology typical of the Christianity they have been confronted with over the centuries, and I do not find his assertions corroborated by the other theologies studied here. This raises the interesting topic of how, in the face of historic change and contemporary theological pluralism, one can identify what is "still authentic" in a religion. Modern Judaism faces this issue most poignantly with regard to its central affirmation, that God gives us law. Christians and Jews might well find it fruitful to exchange methodological experience on this matter.

Moltmann accepts as a premise of his theology the unredeemed state of the world despite the first coming. He then sees the difference between Judaism and Christianity arising from their divergent doctrines as to how the awaited fulfillment will be brought about. "Does redemption depend upon the repentance of man? If it does, redemption will never come. If it does not, it seems to be irrelevant to men. The Jewish answer could be described by saying that God forces Israel to repent through suffering. (Note 41.) The Christian answer is that God brings the sinner, whether a Jew or a Gentile, to repentance through his own suffering in the cross of Jesus. The ultimate difference between Jews and Christians lies in the attitude to the crucified Christ. For Christians, this must also bring about a break-through in the direction of messianic expectations and questions . . ." (p. 102).

Jews obviously do not share Moltmann's pessimism about the possibilities of the turning. People can and should repent; such is the everyday anticipation of the Messiah in which a Jew lives. If people do not, then there is a Jewish tradition that God will cause them to suffer so that they do repent. I understand Rabbinic teaching on this score to be framed in the typical dialectic of Covenant faith (1973b, pp. 25ff). That is, redemption may come from Israel's action—turning—or God's action—forgiving them out of pure love. And some rabbis, unhappy about unrelieved dialectical tension, have God give them a reason to turn so that God can reward their turning with redemption. (The dialectic is properly described in Moore, 1932 II, pp. 350–351.) One may then add to the Jewish "optimism" concerning humanity's power a correlative optimism about God's will despite human failures. I must, however, make it perfectly clear that we, having experienced suffering most intensely, do not see it as a *necessary* means of bringing redemption. We do not seek further suffering and we ask that all who connect suffering with redemption apply that doctrine to themselves and not to us.

The division between Jews and Christians is not then the Christ but, consistent with Moltmann's thinking, Christ crucified. Moltmann is eloquent in his use of this symbol to identify the Church's duty in the present historical situation. As the crucifixion shows the ultimate acceptance of the outcast, so Christianity must now stand in judgment over the laws and structures of our society. It should identify with all those whom our social order exploits and rejects (pp. 176ff).

I do not think it will be useful to discuss the ethics Moltmann derives from his symbol. As always with theologically grounded ethical theories the same symbol can produce divergent interpretations, thus complicating the problems of interreligious discussion. Instead, I wish to discuss Moltmann's understanding of what it meant in ancient Judaism when Jesus was crucified. Moltmann argues that a Jew who was hung "was rejected by his people . . . and excluded from the covenant . . . Anyone who, condemned by the law as a blasphemer, suffers such a death is cursed and excluded from the fellowship of God" (pp. 128–134).

I do not see how Moltmann can justify this assertion. He contends that by Jesus' placing himself above the Torah by for- giving sins, he committed an unforgivable offense for which the Jewish leadership tried him and found him guilty. The obvious problem with this charge is that from the Gospel accounts we cannot be certain what Jewish laws, if any, Jesus broke. Molt- mann explains, "This is not the blasphemy of cursing God, ac- cording to the law, but the blasphemy of self-deification" (p. 129). This is so obviously his introjection into the texts that Moltmann is forced, in his note 41, to suggest that the early Jew- ish law on blasphemy must have been much wider than that stat- ed in Mishnah Sanhedrin 7.5.* That text gives so narrow a definition of blasphemy that Jesus did not transgress it. Recog- nizing this Moltmann says the present wording probably reflects a later Jewish reaction to Christian claims. I know no competent scholar of Rabbinics who has ever made such a claim. Moltmann cites no Jewish student of this material in support of his conten- tion that the Mishnah was purposely revised to make Jesus ap- pear innocent of blasphemy.

Similarly, the notion that one "hung from a tree" is "cursed of God" cannot mean to a Jew, as far as I know, that such a per- son "was rejected by his people . . . and excluded from the cov- enant" (p. 33). We do have the usual problem here with the late date of the editing of our Rabbinic sources, but there is good continuity between the Rabbinic and the biblical material. Cap- ital punishment does not make one less a Jew. Rather, suffering and death are seen by the rabbis as having an atoning power (Moore, 1932 I, 546). True, in the case of hanging alone (one of the four kinds of capital punishment mentioned by the rabbis) the Torah calls the hanged one "cursed of God." The phrase is unique in the legal literature, and since the Bible uses the same

---

* "One is not held liable as a blasphemer until one explicitly articulates the Inef- fable Name."

noun in figurative as well as literal fashion, I do not see that we can insist on what it means there. Plainly the text says that a hanging body is to be taken down before night. But though the hanging may admit of several interpretations we may draw some relatively unambiguous conclusions from what is then done with the executed one's body. As the New Testament accounts show, Jesus' corpse was treated with customary religious respect. If the hanged one were "rejected by his people . . . and excluded from the covenant" the Jewish laws of honoring the corpse would most likely not have been applied to it. It seems far more consistent with biblical and Rabbinic tradition about the unbreakability of the Covenant and God's forgiving nature that Jesus, an apparent sinner, died a degrading but atoning death, remaining a part of his people's Covenant with God through it all.

The issue at stake here is not a technical point of law but the very basis of Moltmann's validation of Jesus' Christ-hood. Moltmann, conceding the unredeemed quality of our world, wants to create a dialectical christology, in which God reveals the truth through the opposite of God, the foresaken and despised Jesus. This causes him, to my mind, to exaggerate greatly. I find such overstatement a common problem with thinkers who work dialectically. If the salvation they promise is to be cosmically significant, the ills they are reversing must be hellishly intense. In Moltmann's case Jesus' situation as the crucified one must be utterly opposed to our expectations of a Messiah so that when its dialectical opposite is revealed it may claim ultimate worth and value. I find this recourse to hyperbole a major problem in Moltmann's treatment of the cross and a weakness in the christology he derives from it.

If we grant that Jesus' misery in his crucifixion qualifies him dialectically to open our way to God, Jews can think of others who have lived who are far more entitled to the role of dialectical Messiah. Jesus suffered a day—Jews at Auschwitz lingered for months before being sent to a gas chamber. Jesus had disciples who may have deserted him but who knew him and could tell his story—the Jews of the Holocaust died anonymously; we do not know most of their names to this day despite three decades of research.

Not only are such comparisons unbearable, I do not think they are useful. If God is truly revealed by God's opposite, is the essence of Godhood power and thus is its antithesis powerlessness? Or is God not, in biblical terms, more positively described, say as the Holy One? Hence God's opposite would be the Profane One, the active agent of evil acts. This, I take it, is the root religious sense of the reality of the Devil—and there is some truth to the thesis that God is revealed in what we know to be the Devil. But surely we would not accept a dialectic which argued that the Devil is the Christ. Obviously Moltmann would insist at this point that analogical reasoning be brought into play and the Devil-as-Messiah thus be disqualified. All I have tried to do by this *reductio ad absurdum* is to indicate how limited a reliance may be placed on a dialectical method. The fundamental question is logical. How is it possible to construct a coherent argument when "a" is sometimes known by the "a-like" and at other times known by the "a-opposite"? Indeed, as I sought to make clear in the argument about the extent of Jesus' abandonment or for the Devil as Messiah-candidate, how can one hope to find the opposite of a thing so as to define it in negation unless one knows the thing itself in advance? To my Jewish sensibilities Moltmann has begun with his symbol—Christ on the cross—and sought a new way to make it acceptable. I believe the logic of his argument too weak to permit one to trust the conclusions reached by means of it, even as I find the substance of his contention inconsistent with what I know of Judaism.

I also have problems with Moltmann's understanding of God in history as revealed through Jesus. The crucifixion shows that God loves the godless, that grace alone makes for righteousness (p. 176). In Jesus a new sense of the right is created in which executioners and the executed are finally all one (p. 178). ". . . only in the question of righteousness in suffering the evil and misery of the world of man does one, in my view, come up against the abiding question of apocalyptic which cannot be settled, and the answer of Jesus and his history, the scandal of which cannot be laid aside" (p. 177). Jesus goes to the cross to show what happens to the kingdom in this world (pp. 184–185). If, then, what is new in the Christ is that acts of righteousness mean no more than acts of sin, if suffering and lowliness are our chief virtues, if being out of power is a condition of salvation, then the old passivity and cheap grace of dependent Protestantism is back in a way unthinkable of the author of *Theology of Hope.* I assume, then, that this statement of Jesus as the model of our enduring rather than changing the world must be balanced by some analogical, activist understanding of Christian duty and that this is but one aspect of Moltmann's christology, one engendered by a time when the possibility of social change was quite low.

The final matter in Moltmann's christology calling for Jewish comment is its heavy emphasis on the Trinity. This is accompanied by a continuing polemic against monotheism. "The more one understands . . . the cross as an event of God the more any simple concept of God falls apart" (p. 204). Monotheistic notions are associated with domesticated, "bourgeois religions." "Christianity cannot therefore any longer be represented as a 'monotheistic form of belief' (Schleiermacher). Christian faith is not 'radical monotheism'" (p. 215).† "In practice, however, the religious conceptions of many Christians prove to be no more than a weakly Christianized monotheism. However, it is precisely this general monotheism in theology and the belief of Christians that is involved in a crisis of identity. For this general religious monotheism is a permanent occasion for protest atheism and rightly so" (p. 236). Moltmann's argument for the Trinity is so strong that he feels constrained to ask himself why he speaks of "God" at all, and responds, "I think that the unity of the dialectical history of Father and Son and Spirit in the cross on Golgotha, full of tension as it is, can be described so to speak retroactively as 'God' . . . [not a] nature or a heavenly person or a moral authority, but in fact an 'event.'" This leads on to "In that case, is there no 'personal God'? If 'God' is an event can one pray to him? One cannot pray to an 'event.' In that case there is in fact no 'personal God' as a person projected in heaven. But there are persons in God: the Son, the Father and the

† Note once again Moltmann's use of a dogmatic form of address to convey "I believe."

Spirit. In that case one does not simply pray to God as a heavenly Thou, but prays *in* God . . . One prays through the Son to the Father in the Spirit . . . Only in this way does the character of Christian prayer become clear" (p. 247).

Reason is still involved in this statement but only in drawing forth the systematic entailments of accepting the crucifixion as the occasion on which God, in full Divinity, communicated the supreme religious truth to humanity. For all its rational elaboration, therefore, Moltmann's doctrine of the Trinity is a statement of his faith. He has tried to make its nature clearer to the nonbeliever, but this is far different from an argument that would seek to lead skeptics to belief or convince them of this Christian truth. Jews could discuss with Moltmann whether Jewish monotheism, asserted in biblical-Rabbinic piety, if in modern terms, is subject to the same strictures he uses against the monotheistic God of the philosophers (pp. 214ff). And if the effect of concepts of God on social behavior were jointly a significant value, the parties in discussion could contrast the ethical entailments of describing God as the Trinity of the crucifixion with those of the God who gives Torah. Yet when it comes to a direct confrontation between Christian Trinity-monotheism and the Jewish sense of God as one, I think we can proceed only on the phenomenological level. In Moltmann, as in Rahner, it is not quite clear how or where reason and faith intersect, or, in their redefinitions, function for public as well as private communication. One of the potential benefits of discussions with them would be to see how each faith, in relation to its basic affirmations, utilizes this combination of levels of assertion and balances the one against the other.

We have one modern example of such dialogue in difference of theologians who partially affirm yet partially go beyond reason, the exchange of letters between Eugene Rosenstock-Huessy and Franz Rosenzweig in 1916 (Rosenstock-Huessy, 1969). Alexander Altmann, in his essay included in that volume, comments that this correspondence has "rightly been described as one of the most important religious documents of our age. The two correspondents face each other not as official spokesmen of their respective faiths but as two human beings who are

aware of their separateness as Jew and Christian and their one-
ness in Adam . . . [I]t is precisely this informal, personal, and direct character in their meeting which brings out a depth of
thought and a frankness of expression that is unparalleled in the
long history of Jewish-Christian relations. Unlike the medieval
disputations, in which dogma was arrayed against dogma and
verse set against verse, this discussion is a true dialogue . . . It is
also an exemplification of what is called the 'existential' attitude
to theological problems . . . [which] considers its subject from an
all-round human viewpoint, instead of isolating it" (pp. 26–27).
Dorothy Emmett, also writing about their exchange, concurs,
calling this "a profoundly sincere adventure in communication"
(p. 49).

More than three decades have passed since Altmann (1944)
and Emmett (1945) published their articles on this correspondence. Sensitivity to interpersonal openness has become such a
commonplace among us that we have a substantially different
perception of what it means to have "personal and direct . . .
meeting" or "profoundly sincere . . communication." And, of
course, it is over sixty years since the correspondence itself. The
exchange of letters is indeed impressive as seen against the
background of medieval polemics between these two faiths.
Here the virtues of modern civility assert themselves and we find
ourselves in the presence of two cultured gentlemen disputing
their religious differences in full academic dignity and respect.
One's admiration for this tone of mutual regard is heightened
when one knows that Rosenstock-Huessy had converted to
Christianity from Judaism and Rosenzweig himself had almost
become a convert. Rosenzweig therefore confronts Rosenstock-
Huessy as someone who has chosen to remain a Jew and was
seeking a way to live in a newly traditional, newly modern form
of Jewish piety. Each, in explicating his faith, was justifying his
choice and validating his existence. In this context, the exchange
between them is exceptionally interesting.

However, the substance of the correspondence is intellec-
tually disappointing. The writers never clarify where they take
issue with the other's faith or why. We do not discover what they
have learned from their correspondent about his faith. They do

not even deal with the proper uses of reason and faith in understanding their own religion or communicating it to others.
Worse, the tone of their letters is such that, despite personal
statement, there is no interpersonal contact. I have read the letters on two occasions. The first time was in 1945–46 when my
Hebrew Union College roommate, Arnold Jacob Wolf, after
reading Professor Emmett's article in the *Journal of Religion*,
wrote to her to share with us a typescript of the translation she
had made (1969, v). We read and discussed the letters then and
I felt that my inability to see any genuine exchange between the
men was due to my having just begun my graduate studies. I re-
read the correspondence and the surrounding materials after
their publication in 1969. I felt less incompetent then to deal
with their range of reference and innuendo. I still did not find
the correspondents listening to each other. They seemed rather
to be enjoying what they discovered and displayed of themselves
in the presence of a worthy antagonist. To be sure Rosenzweig
had not yet written the *Star of Redemption* nor gone beyond it to
the experience of living as a Jew that occasioned his sort of Jewish theology proper.

This correspondence took place some years before Martin
Buber published *I and Thou.* While it has taken us decades to understand Buber's ideas and put them into practice, they have
revolutionized our understanding of authentic interpersonal
communication. For all that, an I-thou correspondence is still a
great human achievement for friends or lovers. The possibility
of such an exchange between those of different faiths was not
even conceivable until recent days. Yet I-thou polemics are what
we must aspire to if we are to have true human relationships despite profound religious difference. The Rosenstock-Huessy—
Rosenzweig correspondence is of little help to us in seeking
such communication. Roy Eckardt considers it a barrier rather
than a model for interreligious exchange. ". . . [T]he correspondents seem to be competing to see who can win out as a master
of obscurity and turgidness . . . [There is] no warrant at all for
the almost unbelievable opaqueness of much in the letters . . .
Undue idealization has been lavished upon these letters . . ."
(1974, pp. 212–213). The judgment is harsh but inescapable to-

day. It testifies to the long distance we have come in our expectations of one another rather than about what it meant for Rosenstock-Huessy and Rosenzweig to engage each other in what even Eckhardt admits was "pioneering candor." We cannot then hope to follow the example of Rosenstock-Huessy and Rosenzweig if we wish to establish a dialogue over the differences between Christian and Jewish thinkers who have moved beyond liberalism without returning to orthodoxy. The shape of such a post-liberal exchange is yet to be fashioned.

VI. Gustafson: The Christ and Ethics

Thus far we have examined christology as it relates to the doctrine of God. The doctrine of the Christ also has consequences for the lives of those who accept it. In this chapter we shall deal with the relationship of christology to Christian ethics. James Gustafson suggests that it may be useful to examine this matter in terms of three questions often asked in moral discourse: What is "the nature and locus of the good"? What does one believe about "the moral self"? What are the "criteria for the judgments" one makes in the moral situation? (1968, p. 4, cf. p. 1). Organizing his presentation around these questions, Gustafson devotes the chapter "Jesus Christ, the Lord who is Creator and Redeemer" to the first question; two chapters, "Jesus Christ, the Sanctifier" and ". . . the Justifier" to the second question; and the chapters ". . . the Pattern" and ". . . the Teacher" to the last question. In his final chapter he seeks to put these several themes into a coherent whole without being merely eclectic.

The Jewish reader of Gustafson's work is likely to emerge from it with two complementary impressions. First, because of differing responses to the Christ, there is a surprising variety of Christian ethical thinking. Gustafson deliberately eschews discussing the thinkers in terms of typologies and thus cannot be accused of exaggerating their differences by the form of his presentation (p. 5). Much of the diversity one finds in the work of these theologians arises from their disagreement as to where to place the primary emphases in Christian ethics, particularly because the Christ and his work may be interpreted in many ways.

Gustafson thus inadvertently makes it clear that anyone wishing to compare Christian ethics with other views of morality requires substantial orientation to the varied topography of Christian ethical positions. What outside critics might assume Christianity lacks may turn out to be an authentic interpretation of Christian responsibility but one that is not popularly known as such.

The second impression derives from the first. There is an extraordinary disparity between Gustafson's presentation of Christian ethics and the perceptions Jews have had to them in the past century and a half. Jewish spokesmen have almost always identified the ethics of Christianity with the principle of love presented in the two love commandments and the Sermon on the Mount. From the single-mindedness with which Jewish writers have contrasted the inadequacy of love as a basis for human existence with that of justice, one would have thought the former quality was the sole normative content of Christian morality. Gustafson's work shows any such view is simplistic, perhaps even ignorant. Since, from the Jewish side, the debate over ethics has been a critical matter in comparing the value of the two religions, this theme is worthy of detailed examination.

Beginning early in the nineteenth century a denigration of Christian ethics (Protestant ethics is almost always meant) has been central to the defense of Judaism against the appeal of the modernist, majority religion, Christianity. Already in the writings of Joseph Salvador (1796–1873) and Elijah Benamozegh (1823–1900), the first notable modern Jewish polemicists, the standard lines of this attack appear. Christianity is individualistic and other-worldly in its primary orientation. Unlike Judaism, which is social and this-worldly, Christianity has no proper ethical orientation (Jacob, 1974).* These polemical attitudes first rise to the level of serious academic significance in the work of Herman Cohen (1847–1918) the founder of the Marburg school of Neo-Kantianism. Cohen saw Kant, as he reinterpreted him,

---

* This work is useful as a speedy survey of these two authors as well as many other Jewish thinkers who have given some attention to Christianity, but its approach is uncritical and defensive.

providing a rationally valid understanding of humanity's place in the universe. This secular philosophy, which Cohen worked out in the final quarter of the nineteenth century, had religious implications since the idea of God played a central role in it. First in occasional writings and then after his retirement in 1913 in a sustained major treatment, Cohen applied his philosophy to Judaism. He found it, of all historic religions, to be the one that most clearly embodied the neo-Kantian notion of "religion of reason." Cohen saw the special relation between Kant and Judaism centering on Kant's double emphasis, that ethics is a major, distinctive characteristic of human beings and that properly rational ethics takes the form of law. (For one, explicit statement see "Affinities Between the Philosophy of Kant and Judaism" in 1971.)

Both themes were important in Cohen's defense of Judaism against Christian claims to final truth. In the Kantian frame of reference, rational beings would seek ethics, not faith. They would build their lives on a morality of law, not one of love. Cohen, who argued that ethics is the essence of Jewish law, had thus demonstrated the rational superiority of Judaism. It is as useless as it is irresistible to speculate whether Cohen's decision to undertake the academic effort of rehabilitating Kant was not in some significant way due to the usefulness Cohen intuited it might have for a modern Jewish apologetic. Cohen's neo-Kantianism has always been described as straightforward philosophical creativity; yet I cannot read the Jewish essays he based on his philosophy without the sense that their polemic against Christianity, implied or expressed, is highly important to him. To be sure, Cohen has a number of other major intellectual enemies, specifically mythology and pantheism, Spinoza being connected with the latter. But it tells us a good deal about Cohen's attitude that he often links Christianity with mythology and pantheism to expose it as insufficiently rational.

From the late nineteenth century on, the Jewish argument against Christianity was shaped by the Cohenian critique: rational people could not accept Christianity. By contrast Judaism could be seen as the finest exemplar of "religion of reason" chiefly because, in an age of acculturation and secularization, the essence of Torah could be equated with Kantian morality. This construction of reality was so useful to Jews living as a minority in a Christian world that it became the common ideology of modernizing Jews. Though support for neo-Kantian rationality has long since eroded in academic circles, most Jews today still go back to the language of rational religion when they seek to justify Judaism against the attractiveness of Christianity.

Cohen's philosophy was not directly known to most of the Jewish community. Its influence was mediated to the masses by the many Jewish scholars whose attitudes were shaped by study in Germany or by the reading of German-Jewish intellectual works, most of which were strongly influenced by Cohen's ideas. Though the extent of Cohen's influence upon them is debatable, two of the most influential Jewish teachers of the early twentieth century indicate clearly the way neo-Kantian approaches to rationality and ethics shape the common Jewish perception of Christian moral theology. Taking them chronologically let us consider the perceptions of Christian ethics of Ahad Ha-am and Kaufmann Kohler.

Ahad Ha-am was the pseudonym of Asher Ginsberg (1856–1927), one of the classic figures of the East-European Hebrew enlightenment, the *Haskalah* movement. In a series of essays written in the two decades before the First World War he crystallized the ideology that came to be called "cultural Zionism." In opposition to Theodor Herzl's emphasis on political legitimization for the creation of a Jewish state, Ahad Ha-am thought nothing more important than strengthening the quality of Jewish national existence. In the spirit of the folk-psychology of the period, he believed each nation had an individual "soul" that gave its culture a distinctive cast. The Jews were especially gifted, he contended, in spiritual creativity. Being agnostic, he meant this in a secular sense, that the Jews had a talent for ethics and culture. He insisted that Judaism contained a distinctive, naturalistic morality.

While he often referred to this view, his most explicit expression of it came when he contrasted the ethics of Judaism with those of Christianity. It appeared in 1910 in response to the publication by a British liberal Jew, Claude G. Montefiore, of a two-volume commentary called *The Synoptic Gospels*. Monte-fiore's attitude may be gauged from this unusual statement, "if Judaism does not, as it were, come to terms with the Gospels, it must always be, I am inclined to think, a creed in a corner, of little influence and with no expansive power" (Simon, 1946, p. 127). Ahad Ha-am's essay on this matter was entitled, notably, "Between Two Opinions" (the phrase is taken from Elijah's challenge on Mt. Carmel to the Israelites to accept either God or Baal, 1 K. 18.21). Ahad Ha-am's concluding paragraphs indicate how radically he took this matter of distinctive national will and identity. "But every true Jew, be he orthodox or liberal, feels in the depths of his being that there is something in the spirit of his people—though we do not know what it is—which has prevented us from following the rest of the world along the beaten path, has led to our producing this Judaism of ours, and has kept us and our Judaism 'in a corner' to this day, because we cannot abandon the distinctive outlook on which Judaism is based. Let those who still have this feeling remain within the fold; let those who have lost it go elsewhere. There is no room for compromise" (pp. 127–28).

His central contention is that "the Jewish people, in contrast to the rest of the world, has a preference for the abstract ideal in religion and morality" (p. 129). Ahad Ha-am shows how, in contrast to other faiths, this operates in relation to God and, in contrast to Christianity, in the Jewish conception of the Messiah. He contends that the "preference of the Jewish mind [is] for the impersonal" and this is the basis of the distinctive Jewish moral and religious goal. "Judaism conceives its aim not as the salvation of the individual, but as the well-being and perfection of a group, of the Jewish people, and ultimately of the human race" (p. 130). He will not argue that this is a higher value than individual salvation, only that it is distinctively Jewish and is part of "the essential character" of the Jewish people (p. 131). This leads on to a discussion of the differing senses of morality in Judaism and Christianity and a defense of Hillel's negative version of the golden rule. "The moral law of the Gospels asks the 'natural man' to reverse his natural attitude towards himself and others, and to put the 'other' in place of the 'self'—that is, to replace straight-forward egoism by inverted egoism. For the altruism of the Gospels is neither more nor less than inverted egoism. Altruism and egoism alike deny the individual as such all objective moral value, and make him merely a means to a subjective end; but whereas egoism makes the 'other' a means to the advantage of the 'self,' altruism does just the reverse. Judaism, however, gets rid of this subjective attitude entirely. Its morality is based on something abstract and objective on *absolute justice*, which attaches moral value to the individual as such without any distinction between the 'self' and the 'other.' On this theory a man's sense of justice is the supreme judge both of his own actions and those of other men. This sense of justice must be made independent of individual relations, as though it were a separate entity; and before it all men, including the self, must be equal. All men, including the self, are under obligation to develop their lives and their faculties to assist his neighbor's self-development, so far as he can. But just as I have no right to ruin another man's life for the sake of my own, so I have no right to ruin my own life for the sake of another's. Both of us are men, and both our lives have the same value before the throne of justice" (p. 132). Ahad Ha-am then cites two sections of the Talmud in which, in varying ways, the question is raised whether one is obligated to give one's life for one's fellow. (Though one case is clearly undecided in the Talmud, he argues that the rabbis prove his point.) It is a tribute to Ahad Ha-am's influence that the two cases, where one man has a jug of water sufficient to take him but not his comrade through a desert (Bava Metzia 62a), and the question whether one may commit murder to escape a threat to one's own life (Pesahim 25b), became commonplaces in later discussions of the ethics of Judaism.

Two other items in Ahad Ha-am's analysis are worth noting. First, he pictures the Days of the Messiah in terms of absolute, impartial justice. ". . . Judaism . . . looks forward to the development of morality to a point at which Justice will become an instinct with good men, so that in any given situation they will be able to apply the standard of absolute justice without any long process of reflection . . . Personal and social considerations will not effect them in the slightest degree; their instinct will judge every action with absolute impartiality, ignoring all human relations, and making no difference between X and Y, between the self and the other, between rich and poor" (p. 135). Second, he argues that while the Jewish morality of justice can easily be carried over into the sphere of international relations "the altruism of the Gospels provides no sort of basis for . . . [it]. A nation can never believe that its moral duty lies in self-abasement or in the renunciation of its rights for the benefit of other nations . . . Hence Christian nations have not been able to regulate their relations with one another on the basis of their religions; national egoism has inevitably remained the sole determining force in international affairs . . ." (p. 137).

Not only decades but unanticipated historic and cultural changes separate the contemporary reader from Ahad Ha-am. To many modern scholars he ignored the Jewish concern for persons and Judaism's teaching of compassion and love, reworked Jewish teaching in terms of a Kant-like rational ethics, denied such an option to Christianity and ignored all Christian ethical teaching other than Jesus' statement of the golden rule understood as self-sacrificing neighbor-love. Perhaps one may explain his limited purview in this essay by recalling that he was responding to a work on the Gospels and, in general, that the popular polemics regularly directed against the Jews contrasted Christian love and Jewish legalism. As he puts it "That Jewish morality is based on justice, and the morality of the Gospels on love, has become a platitude . . ." (p. 131). When one sees him as polemicist and not as the objective dispenser of abstract justice he calls true Jews to be, we can understand better his limited perception of Christian ethics. It is also somewhat surprising that he does not inquire whether the Christian choice of grounds to distinguish between Judaism and Christianity is correct. In his widely read essay "Slavery Amidst Freedom" he had criticized Western Jews for giving up their independent sense of Jewish values to adopt Christian standards. Here he accepts the Christian interpretation uncritically and seeks to show the superiority of an ethic of justice, though he does not make an explicit statement of judgment. Obviously, if Kantianism is the criterion and Judaism is identified with it, the case for Judaism is not difficult to make.

Ahad Ha'am's ideas were influential not only in organized Zionist circles but, more significantly, among the many East-European intellectuals, particularly the educators, who made ethnic loyalty and cultural creativity, particularly in regard to the Hebrew language, central to their Jewish existence. In America the Reform rabbinate and, some decades later, the Conservative rabbinate disseminated a related sense of Christian and Jewish ethics. Kaufmann Kohler, the author of *Jewish Theology* (original U.S. edition 1917), popularized this position. He had an exceptional influence on American Jewry because his book was the first full-scale English interpretation of modern Judaism, and for nearly two decades Kohler was President of the Hebrew Union College, the seminary for Reform rabbis.

The concluding chapter of Kohler's *Jewish Theology* is entitled "The Ethics of Judaism and the Kingdom of God." It is obviously meant as the climax to all that has been stated before. By contrast, the volume has no section on law, though some aspects of Jewish observance and obligation are mentioned in the last half of the book. This may stem from Kohler's understanding of theology as dealing only with matters of belief or from his Reform Jewish sense that the older understanding of Jewish law was now outmoded. In any case, his general inattention to conduct makes his explicit attention to ethics all the more significant.

Kohler declares, "The soul of the Jewish religion is its ethics. Its God is the Fountainhead and Ideal of Morality . . . Accordingly, the kingdom of God . . . does not rest in a world beyond the grave, but . . . in a complete moral order on earth, the reign of truth, righteousness and holiness among all men and nations" (1917, p. 477). Kohler is convinced that the ethics of Judaism are unique and that this is due, in substantial measure, to the unique capacities of the Jewish people for the life of the spirit. Thus he can say that "the election of Israel presupposes an inner calling, a special capacity of the soul and tendency of intellect which fit it for the divine task . . . [the people] must have within itself enough of the heavenly spark of truth and of the impetus of the religious genius as to be able and eager, whenever and wherever the opportunity is favorable, to direct the spiritual flight of humanity toward the highest and the holiest" (pp. 326–327).

Kohler's treatment of ethics is, from the beginning, comparative and polemical, downgrading in turn, though with various degrees of appreciation, nonreligious, Asian, Buddhist and Hellenic ethics. Though he also utilizes folk-psychology, Kohler rejects Ahad Ha-am's understanding of Jewish ethics. Reflecting his religious, anti-Zionist sense of Judaism, Kohler contends that "In contrast to purely altruistic or socialistic ethics, Jewish morality accentuated the value of the individual even apart from the social organism" (p. 482). From this emphasis on the worth of each individual he develops a polemic against an ethic of love. As in Ahad Ha-am, the argument is carried out in relation to the negative version of the golden rule and the proper interpretation of neighbor love. "Taken in the positive form, the command cannot be literally carried out. We cannot love the stranger as we love ourselves or our kin; still less can we love our enemy, as is demanded by the Sermon on the Mount. According to the Hebrew Scriptures we can and should treat our enemy magnanimously and forgive him, but we cannot truly love him, unless he turns from an enemy to a friend . . . Love of all fellow-men is, in fact, taught by both Hillel and Philo" (p. 485). It is also implied in Deuteronomy and explicit in Rabbinic teachings. "However, love as a principle of action is not sufficiently firm to fashion human conduct or rule society. It is too much swayed by impulse and emotion and is often too partial. Love without justice leads to abuse and wrong, as we see in the history of the Church, which began with the principle of love, but often failed to heed the admonitions of justice. Therefore justice is the all inclusive principle of human conduct in the eyes of Judaism . . . the Jewish conception of justice is broader than mere abstention from hurting our fellow-men. Justice is also a positive conception . . . the very principle of ethics of the Mosaic law, the principle for which the great prophets fought with all vigor and vehemence of the divine spirit [is] social justice" (pp.

485–497). "Judaism cannot accept the New Testament spirit of other worldliness, which prompted the teaching: 'Take no thought for your life, what ye shall drink, nor yet for your body what ye shall put on' or 'Resist not evil.' Such a view disregards the values and duties of domestic, civic, and industrial life, and creates an inseparable gulf between sacred and profane, between religion and culture. In contrast to this, Jewish ethics sets the highest value upon all things that make man more of a human being and increase his power of doing good" (p. 489). Kohler continues in this vein, contrasting the Jewish esteem for marriage and wealth derived from labor with the Christian values of celibacy and poverty. "As has been well said, Judaism teaches a 'robust morality.' . . . Jewish ethics excels all other ethical systems, especially in its insistence upon purity and holiness" (pp. 489–490).

The popular polemics against Judaism that formed the background for the early twentieth-century Jewish writings on ethics have been mentioned above. Kohler also has in mind the attacks on Judaism by contemporary Christian scholars. Internationally known figures, such as Bossuet, Delitzsch, Harnack, Weber and Wellhausen, in their investigations of the origins of Christianity, sought to justify their fatih against its Jewish background. They regularly contrasted the New Testament doctrine of love with the aridity of Pharisaism, the Jewish legalism. Kohler considered it a major responsibility of Jewish scholarship to refute their misunderstanding of Judaism. Since Kohler-like attitudes toward Christianity persist in the contemporary Jewish community, it is important to point out that Kohler was not concerned with theological ethics. Though he wrote a book he called *Jewish Theology*, his interests were primarily historical and literary. He did not consider, therefore, the teachings of Thomas, Calvin, Wesley or Maurice, to mention some of the thinkers Gustafson treats. Their ideas would have made Kohler's Jewish ethics seem less distinctive than he took them to be.

This stream of ideas surfaces most visibly in the contemporary Jewish community in Leo Baeck's essay, "Romantic Religion" (in Baeck, 1958). Since its publication in English, it has been the major document on Christianity before American Jewish intellectuals and it therefore merits our detailed attention.

Baeck declares that there are "two forms above all" in piety and religion and that they are "exemplified especially by . . . Judaism and Christianity. In essential respects they confront each other as the classical and the romantic religion" (p. 189). The latter is characterized as follows: "Tense feelings supply its content, and it seeks its goals in the now mythical, now mystical visions of the imagination. Its world is the realm in which all rules are suspended; it is the world of the irregular, the extraordinary and the miraculous, that world which lies beyond all reality, the remote which transcends all things" (pp. 189–190). Romantic religion is distinctively "feminine . . . passive . . . touchingly helpless and weary; it wants to be seized and inspired from above, embraced by a flood of grace which should descend upon it and possess it—a will-less instrument of the wondrous ways of God. When Schleiermacher defined religion as 'the feeling of absolute dependence,' he condensed this attitude into a formula." As a result, "Romanticism, therefore, lacks any strong ethical impulse, and will to conquer life ethically . . . All law, all that legislates, all morality with its commandments is repugnant to it; it would rather stay outside the sphere of good and evil; the highest ideal may be anything at all, except the distinct demands of ethical action" (p. 192). In a telling aside, oblivious to the fact that Immanuel Kant was not a rabbi, Baeck says, "Therefore the romantic 'personality' is also something totally different from, say, the Kantian personality who confronts us as the bearer of the moral law and who finds himself, and thus his freedom, in being faithful to the commandment" (p. 193). Though Baeck admits that no historic religion is without a mixture of the two types he is contrasting (p. 195), he goes on to identify Christianity as the romantic religion *par excellence*, attributing this to Paul (pp. 196ff). "Later on, the Catholicism of the Middle Ages softened this conception and granted a certain amount of human participation. But Luther then returned to the purer romanticism of Paul with its motto, *sola fide*, through faith alone . . ." (p. 205).

Classical religion is activist and ethical as even the history of Christianity shows. "It is, therefore, no accident that peoples with a live sense of independence have turned, consciously and unconsciously, towards the paths of classical religion . . . The history of Calvinistic, Baptist piety with its affinity to the Old Testament, its 'legalistic' orientation, and its ethical stress on proving oneself, shows this clearly. And it was the same story wherever the social conscience stirred; it, too, had to effect this reversion, for it, too, runs counter to romantic religion. The social conscience finds romantic religion repugnant because it is at bottom a religious egoism . . . [I]n it the individual knows only himself and what God or life is to bring him, but not the commandment, not the mutual demands of men" (p. 211). Thus Christianity has had "calamitous" problems with the theory of work. Both Catholic ethics, because of its dualism of heavenly and earthly vocations, and Luther, essentially opposing lazy monks, demonstrate this difficulty. Calvinism is an exception and Baeck says it was "in this respect, too, returning closer to Judaism" (p. 213). A similar point is scored against the Lutheran division between Church and state. "Much as was demanded of the state ecclesiastically, little was asked from it morally." Baeck admits that episodes of Jewish romanticism also show Judaism making peace with tyrants. Nonetheless, romantic religion by its fundamental concerns fosters social conservatism and thus "The problem of culture cannot be solved under a romantic religion" (p. 214). The exceptions grow in Old Testament soil. "From there, too, came the Protestant social movement. The genuinely romantic Pauline faith . . . can confront a culture only as an outsider without any real access to it . . . This faith cannot as a matter of principle do justice to the tasks which the social conscience imposes on man . . ." (p. 215). The concept of Christian culture does not refute this for it is essentially a result of syncretism, a product of "the desire to fuse everything [which] is characteristic of romanticism" (p. 215). The modern notion of an independent culture is essentially un-Christian. "It was able to prevail only by fighting the Church, the Protestant Church just as much as the Catholic" (p. 217).

After a substantial discussion of the evil effects of romanti-

cism as shown in miracle, sacrament, dogma, priesthood and ec-
clesiatic authority, Baeck takes up the classic Jewish polemic
stance, the defense of justice. In romantic religion justice "is
preserved . . . only as an old-fashioned word: the content is completely different. Veracity and justice as active virtues no longer
have any place in romanticism. For the believer there is no command to do anything . . . Paul merely gave this notion its most
exaggerated formulation . . . Justice is for him exclusively something that happens to man: man therefore need not exercise it;
he only must believe in it. Thus it presupposes as its very condition that the will to be just . . . is negated . . . The whole theology of Paul revolves around this negation" (pp. 240–241).
Though in the face of human need this position was changed, as
in James and in the later teaching of the Catholic Church, Luther restores Paul's transformation of justice (p. 243). "The
Pauline faith deprives ethics itself of its basis . . . Ethics was from
now on reduced to a subordinate, if not altogether superfluous,
position . . . Religion now becomes the opposite, the contradiction of ethics; each excludes the other in principle. Either faith
or ethics! That is the innermost meaning of the fight which Paul
and Luther waged against the 'Law'" (pp. 248–249).

Baeck, who maintains the stance of the impartial, descriptive analyst throughout the work, now seeks to show his openness by a brief discussion of the psychological validity of the
romantic approach (pp. 249f). His intentions are made clear,
however, by his opposition to any efforts to ethicize Christianity.
"Where the Pauline doctrine is ethicized, as happens at times today as a concession to what is felt to be modern, the doctrine is
deprived of its very essence, loses its own character, and ceases
to have its own path . . . Ethical religion is in this context a contradiction in terms . . ." Baeck is so determined to fit Christianity
to his ideal types that he can neatly gerrymander the New Testament record. "Paul himself was still too deeply rooted in Judaism and hence made moral demands time and again. These
demands are genuine insofar as they proceeded from his honest
and deeply ethical personality and from his living past from
which he could never disentangle himself entirely. But they are
not genuine insofar as they did not proceed from his romantic

religion which he proclaimed as that which was most truly his own ... They proceed from his personality but not from his faith, and they constitute the contradiction of his character" (p. 250). So the Church could never make ethical duties more than "a mere appendix of religion" and Protestantism did little better, often giving the civil magistrate the effective concern for the moral realm (p. 251). A polemic on Luther's passivity then reaches its climax, characteristically, in the comment "It becomes quite evident ... how impossible it is to derive Kant from Luther, as a certain construction of history suggests from time to time. For Kant the liberating and redeeming power comes from the Law ... Kant's ethics, almost still more than his critique of knowledge, represents the most extreme antithesis of that which was Luther's certainty ... Kant's philosophy of the Law is the very antithesis of all romanticism" (pp. 254–255).

In the concluding section of the essay Baeck mounts another attack on the possibility of Christian ethics. "In the Church, ethics has basically always caused embarrassment. It was there ... but the faith lacked any organic relation to it ... It was considered antiquated and outmoded, a truth no longer valid, something to which only a relapse to a lower stage could lead back. In spite of all this, the religious desire for ethics has, of course, not vanished in the Church ... But ... this quest was vain, and the lot of ethics ... got lost in mere enthusiasm ... pious prayer in some ... in others ... hollow sentimental pathos; or this path led to the collecting and classifying activity of the casuists." This is his judgment of the Catholics, many Lutherans and most specifically, Schleiermacher (pp. 256–257).

One can detect in the Gospels a genuine ethical and prophetic thrust (p. 261) but Baeck insists this has been a problem to the Church. The Catholics solved it by giving responsibility to the elite. "Protestantism, on the other hand, became utterly helpless at this point" (p. 262). The commands of Christ are then interpreted away. This is carried a step forward in modern New Testament scholarship where the virtues taught by Jesus are expounded at great length with the understanding that in life as opposed to faith the very opposite of poverty, not swear-

ing and not resisting evil are validated (p. 263). This is the sentimental side of Christian ethics; it makes "ethics ... an
experience" (p. 265). Baeck then tries to connect romanticism
and ethical casuistry, claiming that it is "erroneous to associate
it exclusively with Catholicism, as if it did not also have its place
in Protestantism" (p. 268).* Once again the section concludes
with a reference to Kant's conception of morality as the proper
criterion for measuring religious ethics. The essay then turns to
questions of last things and concludes with a final claim for classical religion. In it "longing strives ever again for the goal which
is to unify all men and impels them to follow the commandment
of God: after all, these two things really mean one and the same
thing. For all future is here the future of the commandment, the
future in which it is realized and fulfilled. Perhaps it is this [as
against the subjectivity and self-centeredness of romantic reli-
gion] that we find the most clear-cut difference between romantic and classical religion" (p. 292).

This exposition of Baeck's essay, which summarizes much
of the common Jewish attitude to Christian ethics, should clarify
why the Jewish reader is likely to be shocked by Gustafson's rich
presentation of ethics founded on the Christ. To take one case,
there is a world of difference between Baeck's understanding of
Luther's sense of justice and Gustafson's treatment of the ethical implications Luther sees in Christ as humanity's justifier.
Baeck's performance here can be excused only if one assumes
that his reader knows this is polemical literature that he has
picked up in anticipation of seeing the opponent humiliated.
That sort of debate had supposedly gone out with the Middle
Ages and, in the modern style, Baeck presents himself here as an
impartial scholar. Baeck undoubtedly thought that he was being
objective because he followed an accepted modern methodology, namely typology. Yet the method he adopted enabled him to
ignore all contrary data. He could dismiss contrary appearances
as momentary aberrations from the true types of faith he had in

---

* Baeck's exposition of this casuistry is among the least clear and convincing
parts of the entire essay.

mind. Moreover, because the types inhere in the essence of a religion, the historical cannot truly change. Christianity cannot become fully ethical; Judaism, despite its nonethical law and its
mysticism, has been and always will be an essentially ethical
faith. The discussion seems learned and reasonable; in fact it is
fundamentally dogmatic and arbitrary. We are never told how
one discovers the two types, why there are no more, or why they
have these rather than other possible qualities. Baeck knows and
does not explain. He relies on the sweep of his argument and
the richness of his reference to carry the reader along with him.
It is an odd sort of rationality indeed since no counterargument
is ever possible in such a context. For Baeck to have operated in
this manner seems particularly ironic. He claimed a superior
sense of ethics. Yet he judges with unequal measures, a positive
one for his religion, a negative one for his neighbor's.

One can easily imagine the Jewish community's reaction
were the situation reversed. Suppose a Christian thinker discussed the merits of Judaism and Christianity in terms of a typology of religions that were either neurotic, because they
emphasized law and judgment, or autonomous, because they
centered about love and persons. To be sure, one could say
some positive things about the neurotic personality. Its need for
structure and institution produces stability, its drive to accumu-
late merit produces good works and all of us, in one way or another, are neurotic. One would, however, have to deny it any
genuine association with ethical autonomy, the sort of true freedom which the Christ, as justifier, brings us to release us from
our inevitable, incapacitating guilt. The neurotic, as such, is never truly free and cannot therefore reach authentic personhood.
That would simply be untrue to its type.

I do not consider this appeal to the absurdity of the procedure far-fetched. Baeck identified the Torah and *halachah* with
Kant's sense of law and insisted Jewish obligation was essentially
what was required by the categorical imperative. That is not
what traditional Judaism in the past or observant Jews today understand Jewish obligation to be. Why should my typological
polemicist not be as free to describe Judaism as neurotic depen-

dence on law as Baeck is to make Christianity romantic and
hence a-ethical?†

Baeck's performance makes it necessary to restate the fundamental premise of proper comparative religious study. One
cannot discuss other people's religion until one has come to understand it in a way that they would find recognizable. "What is
hateful to you, do not do unto your neighbor." A reading of
Gustafson's treatment of Christian ethics requires the judgment
that much of what Jews have written on this topic does not meet
this standard.

Let us begin afresh. How does a modern Jewish reader react
to Gustafson's exposition of the ethical entailments of the doctrine of the Christ?

Let us begin by reviewing the structure of Gustafson's work.
It treats three ethical questions: What is the ground of our morals? What is the nature of the moral self? And by what norms do
we make moral judgments? Gustafson answers the first question
by discussing Christ the creator and the redeemer. He answers
the second by analyzing Christ the sanctifier and the justifier.
He answers the third by treating Christ the pattern and the
teacher. He gives his own constructive statement in a concluding
chapter (1968, pp. 240ff).

The Jewish response to the first chapter, about the ground
of our morals, comes easily, for there is substantial agreement in
substance though not in means by which it is realized. Gustafson
delineates the theme this way: "Faith in Christ, the Redeemer
and Creator, makes its greatest difference in *the basic attitude* or
disposition of the moral man." True faith in Christ "is at the
root of the freedom from prescriptive and calculating ethics, of
the openness to the world and its infinite possibility in an affir-

---

† On the problems raised by identifying Judaism with Kantian ethics, see Fox
(1975) and particularly the essay by Aharon Lichtenstein, "Does Jewish Tradition Recognize an Ethic Independent of Halakha?" Particular attention should
be given the resolution of the topic in the penultimate paragraph, 83, where
the imperative attached to ethics is declared to be as authoritative as that of the
halachah but with the critically significant yet unexplained qualification, "in its
own way."

mative, positive outlook, of the permission-character of ethics, and of the concreteness of the moral life" (p. 55). In these words Gustafson has summarized the ethical concern of Karl Barth, Dietrich Bonhoeffer and F. D. Maurice. Speaking for himself, Gustafson opines that "Christ as Lord, as Master, for Christians often does, can and ought to give them a particular perspective on life, a particular posture toward life" (p. 242). The verbal usage, "often does, can and ought," frequently utilized by Gustafson, enables him to show what unites Christians in their ethics while at the same time acknowledging the variety in their interpretations of Christian responsibility. Because Gustafson cannot elucidate all the moral implications of accepting Christ, he proceeds to "isolate a most salient aspect of that perspective . . . to show how it functions in human experience. That aspect is confidence in God, in the goodness of the ultimate power and source of life, and in the power of goodness. This confidence, one readily acknowledges, can be evoked by other than loyalty to Jesus Christ, and indeed, is present in the religious and moral faith that Jesus himself shared as a good Jew" (pp. 243–244).

I think most Jews would share Gustafson's judgment about the fundamental attitude our faith engenders in people. To know that there is a God who rules the universe, who covenants with humanity and, through such relationships creates obligations, particularly moral ones, for the covenant partner, links one's intuition of one's personal dignity with one's need to live ethically. To know that God is good and that people can live by the standards of God's own goodness is to give one incomparable hope and confidence in one's moral striving. (I will discuss below the problems created by human sin.) The theological affirmation as Gustafson presents it and the moral claims that devolve from it seem the same in Judaism as in Christianity and further discussion would more likely produce mutual enrichment than substantial divergence of opinion.

However, if one turns directly to the thought of Barth, Bonhoeffer and Maurice, Gustafson's guides in this area, one discovers that they believe people cannot attain the proper ethical perspective independent of faith in the Christ. They insist that, "the Muslim and the agnostic can be affirmative and concrete" in their moral existence only "because of Christ." The believer says this "from his knowledge in faith" (p. 54). As Gustafson notes, this is a matter of dogma for them and thus a topic that is capable of only the most limited cross-discussion.

From the Jewish point of view, it would help if it were possible to distinguish the two functions of the Christ given in this chapter heading, that is, to speak of the creator as distinct from him as redeemer. The purpose of this suggestion is to clarify the areas of agreement and disagreement. Most of what is said about the ethical implications of humanity acknowledging a Creator-God seems common to both faiths. The difficulty arises precisely when the Christocentric attitude requires that Christ the creator not be separated from Christ the redeemer. Judaism has no difficulty asserting belief in God who created the universe and its inhabitants. It rejects the Christian view of how that God relates to people, enables them to be ethical and responds to their sinfulness, all of which will be discussed below. If creation is necessarily linked to redemption in Christianity then there is no area of easy agreement. Yet to consider the ethical implications of the Christ as redeemer seems to Jews the equivalent of discussing him as sanctifier and justifier and this moves us to the second of Gustafson's questions.

The ethical implications of sanctification have to do with the efficacy of grace, that is what God's grace does "to the self, the personal existence of Christians." Among the explanations of this phenomenon Gustafson gives, largely on the basis of a consideration of John Wesley, Friedrich Schleiermacher and Thomas Aquinas, are: "it frees man from various forms of sin; it gives him a new intention; it motivates his will to do the good; it brings his life under a new law of love; it gives him a new consciousness by exerting impulses and influences on him; it directs him toward his proper eternal end; it writes the law of love on his heart so that he can will to follow it; in the form of love it becomes the form of all the virtues, etc. . . . [G]race 'replaces' or at least transforms the sin of self-centered will, the inertia of sloth, the more-than-cognitive dispositions of the human self. In all of them the possibility of moving toward perfection is affirmed" (pp. 113–114).

Major differences with Judaism surface here. Before turning to them let me first point to some themes in this discussion that seem congenial to Judaism. Gustafson describes Wesley's teaching as "more interested in the moral consequences of Christ's work than in an explication of its theological foundations" (p. 72). This sounds like the balance of concerns one finds in classic Judaism. Moreover, "Wesley is not satisfied to leave much mystery in the hyphen between faith-fruits . . . There are stages, steps, and disciplines on the way to perfection" (p. 73). Wesley and his followers could carry this so far that they have often been accused of falling into an unacceptable works-righteousness interpretation of Christianity. Gustafson carefully defends him against this charge (p. 81), but Wesley is surely one of the most if not the most directly challenged Christian ethicists in this volume (pp. 79–83). Without raising the question of the extent to which Judaism believes works grant righteousness in the Christian sense, Wesley's emphasis on the deeds that sanctifying grace should produce has something of the emphasis on deed Judaism makes primary. In any discussion of Christian and Jewish ethics John Wesley's thought might be a useful, near-middle-ground with which to begin.

Similar convergence-divergence themes may be found in Schleiermacher's concern with the role of the community in developing ethical individuals (pp. 91f), a matter of considerable importance in the Jewish view of things. Thomas has a relatively positive view of people's natural ability to be ethical, though he insists it was lost in the Fall and is restored by the grace of Christ in one's baptism. Thus Thomas sees the Christ enabling people to do works of love and prohibiting them from doing those acts that are not loving. Christians should also, in accord with their restored natures, live by the virtues, intellectual, moral and theological, which are the distinguishing signs of humankind. They are also capable of responding to the ethical imperatives contained in natural law (pp. 98ff). In dialogue with Thomistic ethics Jews might fruitfully compare the virtues Judaism and Christianity have tended to emphasize. Faith, hope and charity are commended by both religions though with somewhat different connotations.

Another realm of possible agreement that might usefully be explored is the level of value each faith assigns to moral action. The Christian doctrine of sanctification entails a transformation of the believer's ability to live ethically. As a result, thinkers who stress Jesus' sanctifying power also have certain behavioral expectations of believers. This allows the theologians to appropriate a good deal of Hebrew Scriptures' positive language about the law though it has, to be sure, been transformed by the sanctification context. For Judaism, while behavior is central, the law has its own devices to counteract legalism. (See Lichtenstein's essay in Fox, 1975.) For all the differences between the two faiths there is then also some similarity between them in this area, though this similarity is sometimes denied by polemicists on both sides. (For a Jewish example see Blank, 1968, pp. 75–84.)

The matter of the overlap between Judaism and Christianity might be illuminated by comparing them to some of the European religions that were replaced by Christianity. That is, how did their Christianization change the ethical standards of the peoples involved? Did this bring them closer or further away, say, from the Jewish expectations of non-Jewish ethical behavior, the seven commands to the children of Noah? Rabbi Menahem Meiri (ca. 1249-1306), the great liberalizer of Jewish legal attitudes toward Christianity, explicitly gives as the grounds for his ruling the fact that Christianity had taught the heathens significant ethical limits* (Katz, 1962, p. 115).

Yet major differences remain to divide the religions. The chief of these would seem to be the Christian insistence that sanctification, the enablement of the human will to function ethically, comes through the Christ alone. Aside from the question of mediatorship, which has been discussed above, two significant issues would arise here for a Jewish believer. The one concerns the condition of unredeemed humanity, the other the efficacy of faith in the Christ.

The doctrine of sanctification draws much of its power from

---

* For an argument that Judaism finds its most significant ally in Christianity as both now face the threat of the paganization of contemporary culture, see Borowitz (1969).

the contrast of people's redeemed state to the one in which they were previously, the state of original sin, that incapacity to do the willed good described so notably by Paul. What puzzles Jews about this teaching is that they do not find themselves or other non-Christians as powerless to effectuate the good as Christian theology makes them out to be. As evidence they would point to "the righteous among nations" who manage to live lives of high ethical quality without benefit of the Christ, some surely rising to the level of saints. In Judaism, with its teaching about God's covenant with the children of Noah, humanity, for all its predilection to sin, retains considerable moral capacity.

On this score, Judaism has been attacked for not taking human perversity seriously enough. When today one reads the liberals' optimistic estimates of humankind—Leo Baeck's insistence in the *Essence of Judaism* that Judaism is a religion of ethical optimism quickly coming to mind—and remembers that much of it was written in German, one shudders and must grant some measure of justice to the charge. Experience has altered our perspective. Having lived through the ugly history of recent decades, contemporary Jewish thinkers have given up a previous generation's vision of humanity progressively nearing the Messianic age. In its place they have sought to restate in some modern fashion the Rabbinic teaching about the power and persistence of the evil urge in people. One major Jewish responsibility in a discussion about people's need for sanctification would be to set forth the new Jewish teaching about an unredeemed humanity's ethical capabilities. Despite our fresh respect for the human will's urge to do evil, I feel certain that we would reaffirm our view that people need no Christ to make them ethically competent. In that sense our Jewish "optimism" about humanity remains intact. But let us postpone considering how the divergent views of the nature of humankind might best be approached until we have looked at the other issue in dispute between the faiths.

The point made above about the effect of the conversion of the pagans should make it clear that Jewish thinkers are unlikely to question Christianity's power to alter human behavior significantly. What is disputed are the claims made in the doctrine of sanctification that baptism effectuates a radical change in human nature and that such an alteration of the self can come about only through the Christ. Here the average American Jew will undoubtedly think of the extravagant claims made by Protestant preachers for the transformation effected by conversion. It will then first be important to clarify to what extent Christians expect faith to remake character. Jewish hearers will tend to be skeptical about such claims. They will not deny that conversion can produce extraordinary behavioral changes. Yet Jews will understand this the way many secular students of psychology do. They see conversion as a general human experience when, under extreme emotional stress or peak of emotion, a sudden reshaping of the personality takes place, often with lasting effect. Psychologists believe such characterological events occur in many social settings. Naturally religious contexts tend to be conductive to such happenings, particularly when, as in evangelical Protestant communities, conversions are sought, expected and strongly prompted. Jews will be skeptical, then, that the Christ effects the change rather than the person's mood and the social situation.

There is also a social-historical dimension to this Jewish doubt. On the everyday level, Jews do not find believing Christians living with such moral excellence that they must have been energized by a special, sanctifying power. We know that many Americans are unchurched and others have been unbaptized for a generation or more, limiting the number of true Christians severely. Nonetheless, were the sanctification doctrine descriptive of reality, we should be able to see around us an ethical elite, the superior quality of whose conduct derives from the Christ's transformation of their lives. There are many splendid Christians and some churches do acts of high ethical value. But if Christ sanctifies Christians in the uniquely empowering way theologians claim he does, the effects are not visible to Jewish eyes and they have not been for many centuries. When Christians begin to talk about sanctification opening people to unprecedented ethical capacity, Jews begin to think about crusades, expulsions, the Inquisition, ritual murder charges, pogroms and the Holocaust. Jews cannot understand the Christ as sanctifier since they have not seen and do not see him operative in this way in Christian lives. By contrast, on any number of ethical counts—alcoholism, divorce, crimes of violence—Jews find their statistics extraordinarily better than that of American Catholics or Protestants. This is a matter of considerable pride to most Jews and quite likely the rock of their polemic confidence in discussion with Christians: Jews live more ethically than Christians do. Though the reasons for our skewed statistics may by now be more rooted in Jewish experience than in Jewish belief, most Jews are convinced that, on the whole, Judaism, with its emphasis on action, disposes one to behave better than Christianity with its emphasis on faith. This is one reason why Jewish polemicists against Christianity commonly prefer to join the debate on the issue of ethics.

What has happened in this discussion, however, is unprecedented in the various topics raised in this book. A theological difference has now been approached from the vantage of its empirical effects. If allowed to stand, this move would for the first time provide a basis on which a direct confrontation of the religions could not only be held but, theoretically, resolved. The social scientist would then in all likelihood become the arbiter of theological debate. However, that unlikely result is precluded by most modern theological positions, even where practical effects are expected from religious beliefs. Few theologians, Jewish or Christian, will permit the validity of the faith they advocate to be determined by any measurement of behavior. Gustafson, for example, is careful to avoid making any empirical claims and opens his summary with a series of behavioral disclaimers. If one "asks for historical evidences that the morality of Christians has been demonstrably better, more humane and in actuality superior to the morality of other men, one's honest answer is at best ambiguous . . . No alert Christian needs to have eminent theologians raise the issue for him. Most Christians are readily put to shame by other men whose moral lives have brought the well-being of men into existence far beyond the measure of the efficacy of the activity of Christians. St. Paul speaks for all when he is aware of the good that he does not do, and the evil that he would not do which he does. Christians are in no position . . . to make a case for the Christian faith on the grounds of verifiable evidence . . ." Yet this is not to say that Christianity has nothing to do with one's life in general and one's ethics in particular. "But even those who warn against claiming too much, in their own ways wish to make some claims for a morality that is peculiar to Christians . . ." This concludes by a modest yet substantial statement of his aim. "I propose to explore a way of interpreting and explicating Christian moral life, regarding particularly some of the differences that faith in Jesus Christ *often does make, can make* and *ought to make* in the moral lives of members of the Christian community" (pp. 238–240).

Most Jewish theoreticians would find Gustafson's stance reasonable. While Jewish apologists often contrast the behavior of their people to that of their neighbors, I know of no Jewish theologian who has considered that sufficient proof that God gave the Torah to the people of Israel. One rather finds Jewish writers regularly lamenting the frightening gaps between Jewish expectations and contemporary Jewish practice. At the same time, they are confident that Jewish believing effects Jewish living. Hence they find themselves, particularly in the area of ethics, in something of the same no-man's land of expecting yet not finding empirical consequences, in which their Christian colleagues stand. Both groups might benefit from exploring the ways in which they believe doctrines influence behavior and remain valid no matter how their coreligionists actually live. At the same time, Jewish participants in such a discussion would most likely want to claim that, to some significant extent, behavior is a test of the value of a faith and it should be interesting to see how far they can conscientiously press this point.

If, however, the empirical level of discussion is ruled out, it is difficult to see how there can be direct debate on the issues of the impaired moral power of non-Christians or on their need for the sanctifying power of Christ. We are at a level of so fundamental a perspective or intuition that only phenomenological exchange or the logical examination of entailments seems possible. Strangely enough, though we wish to speak of the nature of people who stand right before us we find we have the same problem of communication we had in relation to doctrines concerning the God who far transcends us.

The consequences of seeing Christ as the justifier bring us to a different ethical context. "The concern for most theologians who think in these terms is basically a religious one and secondarily an ethical one . . . What is required is not works but faith . . ." (p. 118). Thinkers like Martin Luther, Reinhold Niebuhr and Rudolf Bultmann, who are discussed at length here, "claim less, or at least different things, than do writers discussed in the previous chapter (on sanctification). None of them delineates a theory of the virtues . . . None of them differentiates grades and types of sins . . . Yet none of the writers is prepared to say that the grace of God . . . makes no difference at all in moral life" (p. 147). We must now consider that stream of Protestant ethics, so heavily attacked by Baeck, whose admonitions Gustafson puts this way: "Be freed from legalism." "Be free to love freely; be free to face moral issues in their own terms; be free for the future; be free to be pragmatic" (p. 118). Gustafson discusses Luther as an example of one who believes that Christ's liberation of people means that they "can go beyond doing freely what the law requires in personal relations to genuinely new and healing acts of love" (p. 119). He uses Bultmann to show how freedom from the law is understood as freedom from one's past so that one is now radically, existentially open to the present and hence the future. Neibuhr is utilized to illustrate the dialectic of Christian freedom in which those who are redeemed remain confronted with sin and evil so "that the moral life of the Christian is always a struggle against them" in a quite pragmatic and unpredictable way (p. 119).

A number of themes previously discussed arise in connection with the material that focuses on justification. Once again there is a difference of opinion with regard to the human condition without the Christ. Humanity is considered so flawed by sinfulness that it cannot be ethical. God is considered so judgmental that nothing human beings can do will appease the divine wrath. Fortunately God in abundant love sends the Christ to atone for humankind's sinfulness. People, having been convicted under the old law, are now free to make God's will their will in a way they never could before. Thus the debates about God, humanity, sin, atonement, mediatorship recur in connection with the doctrine of justification. Two new questions also arise here, one somewhat minor, the other quite major.

To the best of my knowledge there is nothing in the classic Jewish tradition that corresponds to the personal, subjective effect which the Christ has as sanctifier and justifier. The one internal matter on which Rabbinic Judaism laid stress—setting aside momentarily the virtues, theological, intellectual and moral—was the "turning," repentance, as discussed above. Judaism felt people could do what they had been commanded to do and when, in actuality, they had not done so, they had the power to make such atonement as they required and could expect that God would accept it. Birth bestowed freedom and later sin never completely obliterated it. Freedom was fulfilled through obedience to Torah, whether as stated law or open teaching. On this topic liberals like Baeck, while somewhat overenthusiastic in their Kantian appreciation of freedom, reinterpret traditional Jewish teaching in what seems to me a reasonably appropriate way (Baeck, 1961, pp. 166–171).† Thus there should be considerable value in discussing the kinds of freedom the two religions discern in people. Once it is clear that Christian freedom is not anarchic and Jewish freedom not destroyed by obedience to the Torah, some common examination of liberty and its proper constraints might prove valuable.

What remains as the key difference between the faiths in this regard is the necessity of the Christ to make our freedom effective. For the theologians discussed in this and the previous chapter (on sanctification) the Christ seems the exclusive medium of human liberation, with Niebuhr, perhaps, excepting the Jews from this generalization.

Gustafson's own position with regard to humankind's need of Jesus the Christ is not unequivocally clear. He discusses the source of our freedom in two sections of his concluding state-

† A similarly positive statement of the Jewish understanding of human freedom, though now given an existential interpretation, is found in the thought of Martin Buber (e.g., 1948, pp. 18, 32f).

ment. The one has to do with the self's dispositions, the other with its intentions. In neither analysis does he clarify the connection between the Christ and the aspects of the personality he alludes to and illustrates. He speaks of "characteristics of the Christian life" (p. 249). Thus hope is "worthy of the gospel of Jesus Christ" (p. 250). It is "grounded in trust in the goodness and power of God" (p. 251) and is a disposition "that comes into being through faith" (p. 252). Freedom, too, is "part of the manner of life that is worthy of the gospel" (p. 253). As christological a statement as we find in this analysis is "Cowardice is a form of bondage from which Christ has set men free" (p. 254). A page later this becomes "loyalty to Jesus Christ, gives, can give, and ought to give [the Christian] a freedom from excessive scrupulosity. In his confidence in God and his goodness. . . " (p. 255). The phrase "loyalty to Jesus Christ" is often correlated with faith in God's goodness and to this extent a christological motif undergirds the discussion of intentions (pp. 256ff). The Christ functions in the ethical life of the believer "as sources of illumination even before clear moral intentions are stipulated." This rather indistinct picture seems deliberate. Gustafson comments, "The way one moves from basic Christian beliefs to moral intentions has not been the subject of much analysis . . . I believe that it is fruitful to say that certain intentions are *in accord with* or *in discord with* the beliefs of the Christian . . . or *consonant with* or *dissonant with* . . ." (p. 261).

Does Gustafson then believe that the Christ is indispensable to attaining proper human freedom? For a book whose central theme is the Christ's effect on the moral life, Gustafson says very little about what the Christ does for us, a theological reality, as distinct from his discussion of what our believing in him does for us, a psychological matter. Perhaps Gustafson simply takes the sanctifying and justifying work of Jesus of Nazareth for granted. But to one who is not a Christian believer Gustafson's account says only that belief in the goodness of God confers a sense of self that powers a moral life. As Jews see it, one does not need the Christ to achieve this state, only the cosmic perspective that Christians happen to get through Jesus as the Christ. Jews would then want to inquire about the ways in which

Christians think the Christ functions uniquely to empower the moral life or whether he is understood as the particular Christian symbol through which a universally available ethical enablement is grasped. Obviously, affirming the particular or the universal position alters the nature of the discussion between Jews and Christians. The assertion of uniqueness, if it is made in a fideistic way, delimits discussion. The universal assertion, by contrast, opens possibilities for exploring how the two faiths perceive what both agree is the ethical capacity all people can, ought, and often do have.

Because Gustafson's own doctrine of the Christ is somewhat unclear one cannot debate with him the major issue Jews would raise with the justification theologies of Luther and Bultmann, namely the place of ethics in the life of faith. Reinhold Niebuhr will not appear in this confrontation, appropriately enough, on pragmatic grounds. Though Niebuhr stresses the primacy of faith, his consequent move into life was so speedy, activist and socially oriented, that the objections raised below seem inappropriate to his case. How Niebuhr derived his moral involvement from his theological underpinnings remains an intriguing puzzle to his Jewish admirers. But Niebuhr always insisted that he was primarily a Christian ethicist, not a theologian.

Jews see the issue this way: if ethics are a secondary consideration, they cannot then function properly. Commandment is the single most significant link between God and humankind in the Bible. Faith and trust in God, the knowledge of God, the love and fear of God, and other such subjective aspects of religiosity are valued and commended. None is as frequently mentioned when God speaks to the children of Israel as the details of what God wants them to do. The singleness, the dominion, the holiness of God are all closely connected with God's right to command and our need to do God's will. Jews testify to the reality of God by being faithful to the commandments as they face the challenges of the everyday. From this perspective, to soften the ethical demand or qualify in any way is to demean God's sovereignty and to lessen our reflection of God's image. To be sure, Torah is wisdom and prophecy as well as commandment. It in-

cludes the openness of the teaching (*agadah*) as well as the specificity of law (*halachah*). While Judaism is far more than pious
doing, acts are its unqualified primary interest as its basic response to the sovereignty of God.

This root Jewish concern explains why nineteenth-century
Jewish thinkers found Kant's philosophy congenial. Kant taught
that the ethical had the form of a categorical imperative. This
seemed to say in modern, abstract language what the Jewish tradition had always implicitly affirmed: ethics takes the form of law
and is an unconditional command. Thus Christianity, in making
ethics second to faith and justification, breaks the categorical
quality of the imperative. What is unqualifiedly demanded of the
Christian is faith in the Christ. As Gustafson shows, Christian
thinkers will then insist that, in varying ways, ethical existence
will result. Yet from the Jewish and the Kantian point of view
this Christian compromise with the priority of ethical commandment vitiates its essential nature, which all the afterthoughts
about the importance of moral action cannot restore. Gustafson
says once "The Christians life is not less moral because it is not
primarily moral" (p. 183). This, precisely, is the issue Jews
would wish to argue, but Gustafson neither expands on this assertion nor returns to it elsewhere.

Something also must be said about the practical effects of
subordinating ethics to faith. Christianity needs no instruction
from Judaism on the human proclivity to sin. Yet making ethics
less than the most important thing seems to us to provide a
ready rationalization for the human will to be less than ethical.
Here the Jewish empirical argument will be reasserted. Jewish
polemicists will insist that Christians behave less well than Jews
on many counts because their religion does not stress good
deeds as much as Judaism does. Were ethics of greater importance to Christianity, the Jewish argument goes, Christians
would be more ethical.

Jews almost invariably continue their polemics with an attack on Christian ethics for its relative lack of content. Since the
norms of Christian ethics are Gustafson's third issue, they will
be discussed later. What may no longer be postponed is mention of contemporary doubts about the tacit premise of the Jew-

ish argument advanced above, that Jewish law is essentially ethics or closely to be identified with ethics. Now that some decades have passed since the Jewish neo-Kantians made this thesis widely accepted among Jews, a revisionist view of the matter has appeared and received substantial credence. The extent to which Judaism has an ethics in the sense that Christianity does, and the relationship between Jewish law and the ethics of Judaism, remain to be clarified. This second matter will be raised again in connection with our later discussion of norms.

Philosophers have generally thought of ethics as a rational, nonreligious activity. Their sense of ethics as religiously neutral may open up new possibilities for interreligious confrontation, in this case on the nature of the moral self. There is much about the philosophical understanding of the ethical that would be of interest to both Christianity and Judaism. How should they relate to an ethics which asserts, often by simple definition, that it is independent of God or revelation? What can such ethics teach them about the nature and form of the ethical? A comparative study of the religious approach to ethics, as contrasted to that of secular philosophy, might disclose much about what unites them as religious ethicists and might also clarify their distinctive stands within that position. They clearly diverge with regard to the hierarchical value they assign to ethical behavior. Though they may not be able to debate that issue directly, they can at least clarify for each other the ways in which they seek to compensate for the problems engendered by their primary commitment. How does Judaism seek to enrich the spiritual life of the individual Jew when it stresses action and allows its concern with faith to remain largely implicit in the commandments? What sorts of personal piety does it then create? What does Christianity do to make ethical living fully imperative though not primary in the Christian life? And what special forms of Christian ethical living result from this?

The final theme raised by Gustafson is the Christ as ethical model and teacher. Gustafson divides his treatment of this material between that which centers on how Jesus lived, the Christ as pattern, and what, in a substantive way, he taught. In both cases, Gustafson is at pains to maintain a proper Christian balance between faith and ethics. Again and again he comments that the emphasis now on what the Christian should do must always be understood in terms of belief in the Christ. He even criticizes a number of Christian ethicists for making ethics rather than faith the most important thing in the Christian life.*

Theoreticians of Christian ethics seem to me to face a dilemma. Fixed on one horn is the notion that the Christ has come to free humanity from the law. The thinkers may not then show any trace of legalism, whether by suggesting an independent moral law or ethical rules, or even by turning the words and deeds of the Christ into an objective Christian requirement. Fixed on the other horn, the New Testament and specifically Paul, the great advocate of the new freedom in the Christ, make clear that not every behavior is right for a Christian. Common sense and recent history likewise indicate that characterological anarchy is incompatible with Christian existence. But how can one give direction to Christian freedom without giving rise to the charge of legalism? Will not suggesting a positive content for the Christian life attack the untrammeled liberty that is its very ground?

Gustafson solves this dilemmatic difficulty by using the modern notion of the person. By centering ethics on the sort of self one is, one avoids the problems posed by laws since existentialism has demonstrated that authentic personhood cannot be structured by external rigidities. However, one can indicate something of what constitutes a proper self and in this way point to what a Christian self would likely be and how a Christian would therefore likely act. Gustafson therefore rejects two notions almost totally. First, that the Christ is the Christian's moral ideal and second, that Christian ethics is essentially an imitation of the Christ's self-denial (pp. 159–160, 180–181).

For the same reasons, he is attracted to the suggestion, presented in the names of Martin Luther, Gustaf Wingren and Joseph Sittler that "We are to participate in [the Christ], the engendering deed, and in our own relations to show forth the

---

* His backtracking in the treatment of Christ as moral ideal (pp. 159–160), and his rejection of the teachings of Thomas à Kempis and William Law (pp. 180–181), are particularly noteworthy in this respect.

action of God in man" (p. 171). "Thus we have an ethic closely related to the themes of justification and the new life. But his [Jesus'] effect is to mold our deeds according to the deeds that mold us. As Christ loved us, we are to love; as our needs are met in his acts, so we are to meet the needs of others. We have been freely helped; we ought freely to help. The content of our decision is the stuff of our time and place; we can shape it in obedience and love, in faith and in hope, seeking what counsel we can find from the Bible but also from life. But our actions are not primarily conformations to counsels, principles, goals or even historical persons as life patterns of humility and suffering. They are conformed to what forms them: God's action in Jesus Christ" (p. 176).

I cannot see that more is being said here than was said above in the discussion of justification. The substantive guidance Gustafson offers is so dependent upon the interpersonal relationship between the Christian and the Christ that one who does not share it has difficulty in knowing just what is being proposed. I have no problem appreciating the technical accomplishment of these theologians. They remain true to their primary emphasis on faith and show how it can instruct without creating a legalism of even the most tenuous kind. By scrupulously avoiding any hint of objectifying obligation, however, they seem to me to render the resulting content of their ethics utterly subjective. Thus outsiders can hardly discuss the ethical adequacy or inadequacy of the content to which they point.

By contrast, Gustafson identifies a group of ethical teachers who suggest that Christians will find an appropriate pattern for their lives in the way the Christ's relationship to God was reflected in his relations with people. These thinkers identify the characteristics of proper Christian living, say that the Christ was obedient, suffering and lowly; or that he was "the cross-bearer." Since the theologians he cites are John Calvin, Sören Kierkegaard and Dietrich Bonhoeffer, faith is the context of any statement about the qualities that the Christ showed and Christians should now manifest. Gustafson's point is that their sense of faith has certain activist entailments and grace does not come cheaply.

Gustafson's own explication of this theme demands lengthy citation, particularly since this is an era where Jews are apt to react sharply to Christian claims. He defines the Christian notion of self-denial as "taking the sufferings of others upon oneself, inner if not outer separation from the world" (p. 183). "Self-denial is not necessarily always outward—we are not uniformly called to deny ourselves the pleasure of symphonies or of automobiles—but it is appropriately inward. It is being related to the world in such a way that we both care for it yet are indifferent to it; that we are good stewards . . . External, visible self-denial . . . may also show, in those called to such a life, that lowliness and simplicity are ample and suitable modes of life in faith" (pp. 184–185). "But self-denial includes cross-bearing . . . It is also taking upon oneself the world with its cares and aspirations, its sufferings and its healings, its justice and its victories. It is an inner identification with the downtrodden and disinherited in their struggles for justice and a better life . . . [It] is neighbor-love through inner communion with his concrete suffering and need . . . But it is not only inward. It is outward. Action appropriate to the inner unity is fitting and normal . . . It is not only inwardly costly through the sharing of pain and sorrow, but outwardly costly in the expressions appropriate to the occasion— identification and support of unpopular causes, speaking out against the voices of self-satisfaction and tyranny, taking risks of one's own earthly security and prestige" (pp. 185–186). It is a new life, "a life of freedom from the rigidities of morals and customs, freedom to do the unexpected, to violate the herd morality, to create new good in new forms. The pattern we have to follow is more clearly a pattern of outlook and disposition than a pattern of action . . . Social ethics remains pragmatic to a great extent. But one living in a society with all its closed character is given courage, life, and hope to break through accepted levels of custom and social pattern, to bring new possibilities and life to bear" (pp. 186–187).

From the Jewish perspective these norms seem woefully thin. Perhaps what is at stake between the religions here is what sort of theory may properly be called an ethic. On the simplest level the term may be applied to any standard by which one

judges what one ought to do in a given situation. That is so inclusive a use of the term ethics that, considering the many alternative life-styles currently being promoted as advanced
morality, I do not consider it appropriate in a Judeo-Christian
context. That, in turn, raises some significant questions. How
substantive must one's proposed standard of behavior be to be
considered a Judeo-Christian ethic? What sorts of qualities need
it contain to be an authentic continuator of the biblical attitude
to righteous living? Jews would come to such explorations with a
tradition that emphasized contentful guidance. We will want to
insist that substance as well as motive and form determine a
proper ethic. At the same time, Jews listening carefully to their
Christian colleagues may well learn about the possibility of serving God through an ethic that remains relatively open in content
while giving priority to personal perspective, freedom and the
right ideal.

While the full question of the content of Christian ethics as
presented by Gustafson must await our discussion of Christ the
teacher, some word must be said here about such content as
Gustafson has already suggested. To Jewish eyes it seems overly
passive. Christian obedience seems as closely linked to being
crucified as Jewish responsibility is to doing commandments.
Critics will argue that the Jewish sense of activism is less indige-
nous to the Jewish tradition than it has been made out to be.
One can easily detect in my characterization of Judaism the influence of modern secularism with its emphasis on the self as
moral and political agent. Jews and Christians could beneficially
discuss with one another the ways in which their ethical sense
has benefitted from the challenge of ethical humanism. In this
respect again they share the problem of how much one can
transform an old tradition and remain faithful to it. They will
probably differ as to their sense of how authentic their appropriation of modern activism is (so Baeck's indictment of modernizing Protestants), and how much they (particularly Jewish law)
are able to assimilate the modern concept that self must be self-
legislating. Jews will insist that by contrast to the Christian tradition of cross-bearing, their classic concern for commandment
can easily be extended by the modern notion of activism. The

argument between the faiths would now seem only to be about the proper balance between passivity and activity, both of which qualities each faith affirms.

The empirical level cannot be avoided in this confrontation. Jews have known individual Christians who in their lowliness and self-denial were noble people, even saints. Over the centuries, however, the experience of most Jews with most Christians as persons and with Christian institutions has been of an utter disparity between Christian teaching and Christian behavior, particularly toward Jews. To paraphrase Gustafson, to Jews, Christians and their churches have not, do not and are not likely to care as much for others as they care for themselves, their institutions or their fellow Christians, much less to deny themselves for others or, as the Christ did, to sacrifice themselves for them. They surely have not sacrificed themselves for us. The notion of Christian cross-bearing seems to us to die the death of "a thousand qualifications." By the time Christian teachers are done explaining what it means to take up one's cross and suffer with the Christ one seems only to be authorized to consider it a virtue to endure one's bourgeois troubles. Kierkegaard, for all his lacerating attacks on the self-satisfied Christianity of his time, managed to combine being a knight of faith with living as a Copenhagen dandy. I confess that I have written these last few sentences in some bitterness of spirit. Had even some visible minority of Christians chosen to suffer with their Jewish neighbors over the centuries, I would not react so intensely. Had more than a handful of Christians shown themselves ready to sacrifice themselves so that Hitler's infamy would have its proper Christian protest, I would be less scornful of Christian claims to live by an ethic of self-sacrifice. And I am convinced that my attitudes here reflect what most self-respecting Jews feel but rarely feel free enough to say in public. Two things seem true: empirical evidence is inappropriate to the determination of moral truth; history is not irrelevant to the Christian-Jewish discussion of ethics.

Gustafson approaches this matter as Jewish theologians would do, acknowledging the gap between our teaching and our practice. "The absence of self-denial, of cross-bearing, of lowliness and suffering may indicate the weakness and the sickness of Christian lives. It may indicate that they have a center other than God, other than Jesus Christ . . . [Such people may be] finally culture-centered and self-centered" (p. 184). One cannot help sympathizing, then, with those scientific students of religion who wonder how Jews and Christians can continue to make assertions that are contradicted or very poorly supported by empirical data. Studying ways in which both faiths do this and any differences in this regard would expand our understanding of the logic by which theologians firmly assert propositions that they know have little empirical support. Surely Gustafson's heavy emphasis on the inward side of Christian self-denial significantly stems from a desire to deny in advance the legitimacy of any empirical refutation. He regularly gives more emphasis to what transpires in the Christian's inner life than how conforming one's self to the Christ affects the outer life. With regard to the latter aspect, he can limit self-denial to "those called to such a life." When speaking of cross-bearing he finds it necessary to say that outer action is "fitting and normal" as if the cross Christ bore was not wood but only a distressing mood of conflict, alienation or rejection (p. 185). Apparently Gustafson is concerned here with the Protestant danger of making ethics too objective and systematically reinterprets these ethical qualities in terms of his personalist scheme. This raises the question of what sort of ethics it is that concentrates on intrapsychic matters. No Jew is likely to deny that the religious life manifests trust, confidence and other virtues of piety. The extent to which they comprise the content of our ethic must be considered part of the agenda of differences between Judaism and Christianity.

Gustafson's presentation concludes with his most concrete discussion of Christ as the guide to ethics, namely his role as teacher. For our purposes his discussions of Rudolf Bultmann and Karl Barth may here be omitted as they do not take us beyond issues previously raised. More substantively significant to us are the thinkers who have seen the Christ giving Christians a new law, ideal or norm for their decision-making. With regard to a "law," Gustafson analyzes the debate between T. W. Manson and Hans Windisch. For Manson the only difference between Jesus and his Jewish contemporaries is that "The moral demands of Jesus presuppose a changed nature and disposition in man: they imply a previous conversion" (p. 214). Windisch argues that the antithesis between inner disposition and law is a false one. "It seems probable to Windisch (and with apparent good reason) that Jesus' words that take the form of commands were intended to be commands" (p. 215). Christian ethical writers have regularly taken one or the other point of view. "In main-line Protestantism and Catholicism, the teachings have never received the literal obedience they have got from the radical Reformers. Most churches have not followed the 'higher way' view of exemplary obedience to the teachings of Jesus as their vocations. Yet the idea of the 'new law' has not been abandoned or even neglected" (p. 217). For Catholics it emerges clearly in Thomas's treatment of the new law as that which man, now free to resume his proper nature, can be expected to fulfill (pp. 217f). "What is it, then, specifically that the Sermon on the Mount in particular, orders as the new law? . . . First, Christ commands the will to refrain from the inner acts of sin and from the occasions of evil deeds . . . Second, in acts toward the neighbor we are forbidden to judge him rashly yet also forbidden to 'entrust him too readily with sacred things if he is unworthy.' Finally he teaches us to fulfill the teachings of the gospel, to strive to enter through the narrow door of perfect virtue. Christians are not merely to fulfill these 'interior movements,' but also to take seriously the 'optional' counsels specifically given in the new law" (p. 219). Among Protestants this occurs as the question of whether there is a "third use" (in addition to political and theological uses) of the law, that is, as a guide to Christian living. "Calvin not only had a third use but said it was the most significant use" (p. 220). In this regard he departs radically from Luther. Calvin sees conversion as granting the Christian a better understanding of the law and a greater drive to fulfill it. "Chiefly, the law that forms the Christian moral life for Calvin is the Decalogue" and while he does not give "detailed attention to the Sermon on the Mount or other teachings of Jesus, he does make certain claims for what Jesus Christ has indicated about the law" (p. 221). Calvin believes the Christian should now have a more rigorous awareness of the inner part of action. Thus the command not to murder means not only what it says but that we ought to abstain from all acts injurious to others. Calvin even extends it to include a fully positive connotation. "We should do everything we positively can toward the preservation of the life of our neighbor" (p. 222). For him, the whole law is summarized in the commands to love God and to love one's neighbor.

A second way the Christ might serve to give substantive ethical guidance is by setting the proper ideal for Christians. Manson's statement is cited as characteristic for this view. "The ideal picture of human life which Jesus draws in what he has to say about morals, is a picture of life in the Kingdom of God on earth, life as it may be lived by men who acknowledge one supreme loyalty, in whose hearts one supreme passion burns; and it is only as we hear the call to that loyalty and feel that passion that the moral teaching of Jesus grows luminous" (p. 227). This nebulous if appealing ideal was given substantial content by the social gospel theorists of American Protestantism. They turned what seems to have been spoken essentially to personal situations into a social theory. While not neglecting the need for personal transformation, they believed Christian ethics demanded changing the social situation in full political and economic measure. Walter Rauschenbusch, the best known interpreter of this doctrine, recognized that Jesus inherited a social ideal from Judaism but "he made corrections of the traditional conception so that in his teachings 'we have pure Christian thought and not inherited Judaism' " (p. 228). Against Judaism, Jesus repudiated the use of force; reached out "beyond jingo patriotism toward the brotherhood of all nations"; democratized the despotic possibilities of a kingdom of God by emphasizing service; called for economic emancipation but, more important, spiritual values; discarded utopian values; and concentrated on present duty (pp. 228–229).

There is another American school of Christian social ethics that seeks to make the law of love a norm for ethical decisions and policy-making. In Paul Ramsey "the procedure is to make love 'in-principled,' that is, to find those moral prescriptions that specify the proper inferences from the law of love for gen-

eral problem areas such as war or sexual behavior. These principles in turn function as rules for conduct" (p. 230). For John
Bennett, Christian ethics should try to state "middle axioms" as
a "procedure for moving between love as norm and the com-
plexities of moral existence" (p. 231). For Bennett "The responsibility of Christians, then, is to find the best course of action in
the world in the light of the norm of love, on the one hand, and
the norms that exist in society, on the other." Gustafson considers Reinhold Niebuhr's treatment of love as the "impossible
possibility" related to this approach. Here love functions in
transcendent dialectic with justice to provide for a continuing
Christian involvement in social problems while yet providing a
norm that transcends even the best of immediately desirable solutions.

For Gustafson himself the Christ functions as norm in a
personalistic way. That is, the Christ as person, not his verbal-
izations or actions, is critical for the Christian ethical life. Once
again it is the effect on the Christian's perspective which is de-
terminative. The Christ gives Christians direction. "Direction is
a useful term, since it avoids the connotations of specific compli-
ance to specific percepts, on the one hand, and the reliance on
expressions of attitudes without governance by any objective de-
lineations of proper conduct on the other hand . . . It indicates
. . . a basic intention, a movement in a relatively clear way, toward certain ends. The direction of the teachings can have a validity that is more general than the specific statement made by
Jesus under specific historical conditions that no longer prevail"
(p. 236). The teachings have authority "as relatively precise ver-
balizations about the manner of life and the deeds fitting for disciples of Jesus Christ" (p. 237). In the concluding chapter
Gustafson describes the normativeness of Christ in somewhat
different terms and does so on three levels. First, "Christ provides for the Christian the normative point for the theological
interpretation of what God is willing in the time and place of his
life." Second, the New Testament figure and his teachings are
"the specific instance in which trust in God, and words and
deeds directed toward men find their most perfect correlation
. . . Third, insofar as one's discipleship to Christ is to be the

point around which the being and words and deeds of a person find their integrity, the Christian is obliged to consider Christ as the most important norm among others that are brought to bear in his judgments and actions" (p. 265).

Jews would find it relatively easy to enter discussions of the Christ as teacher. The sort of ethics being spoken of is very much like that Jews are accustomed to, for the theologians are speaking essentially about the content of our responsibilities rather than about the need for or effects of personal change. Gustafson, in passing, makes explicit the difference between this material and what has preceded it. "For all writers who stress the teachings as law in some sense, as for all who view them as the representation of an ideal, or as a moral norm, the place of morality within the Christian life is perhaps larger and certainly more clearly defined than it is for those whose major fear is that morality becomes idolatrous, or falsely believed to be saving" (p. 224). Jews believe they are sufficiently schooled in the evils of idolatry that they do not substitute the law for God, though they insist that, under a covenant, performance of one's obligations is salvific. Nonetheless, this statement makes clear that as Christians become more concerned with the content of Christian ethics the possibilities of discussion with Jews increase. Incidentally, here Gustafson associates an emphasis on the content of ethics with a regard for their place in a Christian existence.

To me, the least substantive of the three modes of seeing Christ as teacher is to see him as exemplar of an ideal, the ideal of the kingdom of God. Since this symbol is common to both religions, one could explore what this meant in the Jewish tradition as it came to Jesus and then see how he and the rabbis transformed it. I would venture the proposition that both faiths share a somewhat similar vision of the coming kingdom though both would agree that its content is not fully explicable. Hence it would be interesting to know to what extent this intuition of the similarity of views is correct and on what basis such a judgment can be made. If I am correct, the groups could also jointly explore the problem of creating new symbolic figures by which to describe what they anticipate. With the failure of most literalist and liberal metaphors, we have almost no evocative terms by which to speak of "the coming of the kingdom." Perhaps earnest cross-cultural dialogue might help us each get beyond the contemporary failure of our imaginations with regard to the *eschaton*.

Some special attention needs to be paid to the question of the social gospel. To Jews, it seems so unique a corporate concern in Christian ethics that we will be quite concerned to know its place in Christian teaching today and the judgment scholars make with regard to its Christian authenticity. Rauschenbush chided the Jews for their having a narrow, tribal attitude to the kingdom of God. But because Judaism was fundamentally concerned with a specific ethnic group, the Jews, it had a major social thrust from its earliest days. By contrast, the Jesus of the New Testament seems to us almost exclusively concerned with the single soul, specifically with individuals coming into the kingdom of God. How Christians make the transition from Jesus' apparent focus on individual eschatological salvation to the proper conduct of societies in history now, is a matter of major Jewish curiosity.

On the whole, Jews will feel we have not yet been given much guidance as to what we ought to do. Rauschenbusch's vision of the kingdom of God was never very clear, and the political and social analysis with which he fleshed it out seems almost outmoded by now. If we seek guidance for our lives we receive much more help from those thinkers who speak of the Christ as a norm. Ramsey, Bennett and Niebuhr all approach this matter by analyzing the Christ's teaching about the proper nature of love. What they refer to is like an experience all humans have known or that Jews referred to when they, Jesus among them, read in the Torah that they were commanded to love God and their neighbor. Hence in a discussion of love as an ethical norm there is a common, experiential base from which to begin the discussion. What makes this groups of thinkers particularly interesting to Jews is their sense of the need for rules, or axioms, or a counterbalancing sense of justice by which to make love work as a norm. Keeping in mind our previous strictures made about keeping orthodox and liberal thinkers in separate categories, it should be fruitful to compare the balance between love and justice and the uses of rules in the two religions. Jewish thinkers have learned much in the past several decades from the writings of Niebuhr, Bennett and Ramsey. How this could take place, though major theological matters separated the Jewish readers from the Christian thinkers, provides a uniquely positive challenge on our lengthening list of desirable interfaith exchanges. A practical matter should also be noted. Understanding the relation of theology to political strategy where ethical issues are at stake should facilitate the continuing cooperation of the two faiths in social matters.

Gustafson's own statement concerning norms does not go as far in providing substance to Christian ethics as do those of the previously mentioned writers. Of his own three aspects of the Christ as norm, the last is purely formal: if one is a Christian, Christ must be his most important standard. Thus we are left with two ways in which Christ functions as the norm: by indicating what God wills for the Christian now and, via the New Testament pictures of him, showing the most perfect correlation of trust and deeds. How the Christ shows one today what God desires of one does not come through to me in Gustafson's admittedly brief exposition (pp. 265–268). Assuming this could be clarified, we might then examine some analogies in traditional Judaism for trying to determine what it is that God wants in a given moment. Admittedly, since the center of the Jewish life is an eternally valid law and teaching, the need for fresh insights into what God presently desires is relatively rare. The theme, however, is not beyond Jewish experience and thus joint discussion.

Gustafson also suggests that Jesus is "the most perfect correlation" of faith and life (p. 265). I have discussed above the Jewish reaction to this claim. Here I wish only to point out that Gustafson's claim seems limited to Christians. In opening his detailed discussion of Christ as norm, he contrasts his view with that of Karl Barth and other such thinkers. For them the Christ "is *the unique* and *only proper* norm for elucidating what God wills in the world" (p. 266). Identifying himself with Catholic thinkers who have been able to discuss certain ethical issues in relative independence of christology, Gustafson then goes on to claim

that "For Christians, Christ becomes a norm . . . a source . . ."
At this point Gustafson is arguing that the Christian needs to
take many factors into account in making a decision, and faith in
the Christ does not exhaust the ethical decision-making process.
But there is an equal emphasis throughout the discussion on
"for the Christian," and this comes to a climax on the penultimate page of the book. Gustafson will make no "claim for the
moral superiority of a Christian" and does not "say that only
Christians can perceive the good or . . . that they perceive it better than others do. Rather [he is suggesting] that those whose
lives are nurtured by the Christian community, who are called to
faith in God through Christ, who commit themselves to discipleship to him are given illumination from Christ in their moral
lives" (p. 270). Gustafson does not explicitly say that there are
other religious norms that might be equally as good for other
religionists as the Christ is for Christians. He does not tell us
that non-Christians with such a norm do not need the Christ.
Yet it would change the discussion radically to know whether he
believes, leaving all other religions aside, that, as many Christians once believed, the Christ still makes claims upon the Jews
and holds open to them a fulfillment they cannot achieve elsewhere. Surely the Jewish-Christian discussion of Christ as a symbol of the proper correlation of trust and deed would be far
different if universal rather than group claims are made for his
status.

Judaism would be most at home in a discussion with those
Christian thinkers, like Calvin and Aquinas, who see ethics as
the appropriation of law, a new law to be sure. Yet what would
then seem like a simple discussion of differences, namely, which
law is the more adequate, cannot proceed on that level. For Jews
the law operates almost naturally, as it were, since the covenant
with humanity is part of the creation and the renewal of creation
after the Flood. (Israel's Covenant is only a special instance of
what all people can know from their own lives without benefit of
conversion or special revelation.) But for all their emphasis on
law, Calvin and Aquinas operate on the basis of a prior condition of faith-grace that alone renders the law properly function-

al. Hence it will not be possible simply to compare content and ignore context.

Nonetheless, some comparison of required action yet remains. What is the law for the Jew and the law for Calvin's or Aquinas's Christian? Where do they converge and where do they differ? To what extent are the divergences easily traceable to different faith perspectives or to what else may they be attributed? It might even be possible to find areas where, in the presence of similar belief, the one faith might show the other how it had developed a sense of entailment unknown to the other. Conversely, it would not be unusual in the study of religions to discover that similar ethical mandates seemed tightly linked to widely different religious foundations. Since for both religions a God not completely available to reason is the ultimate arbiter of ethical validity, these comparative studies could only rarely lead on to a resolution of the different views.

The appearance in Christianity of an ethical sense of law is of the greatest interest to Jews. We would be most eager to know the status of Calvin's and Aquinas's doctrine of law in contemporary Christian thought. Were they, for all their Christian excellence, Judaizers, reversions to a previous state of religious piety? How did they manage to integrate their comparatively great ethical specificity, law, with their concern for the primacy of faith? How does this balance in them compare with the Jewish sense of personal faith as fulfilled in living by Torah, its law and its teaching? Now that our society seems sated by its experimentation with permissivism, is anything like Calvin's or Aquinas's approach to ethics reappearing in Christian ethics?

Yet this chapter cannot conclude without raising some problems about the Jewish side of the dialogue. Just what is meant by Jewish ethics? Surprisingly, there is no good answer to that question. Despite all the pride of Jews about their ethic there has in recent decades been no book of academic quality that has traced its development or delineated its content. Perhaps that is because the previous generation made more claims for Jewish ethics than contemporary thinkers can fulfill. The liberals had said that Jewish law was in essence, if not in all its content, the equivalent of a Kant-like ethics. This idea was extraordinarily appealing, not the least for supplying a modern hermeneutic to validate Jewish practice. Suddenly, the Jewish tradition was seen as a treasure trove of ethical insights. Passover celebrated human freedom and *Shavuot* (Pentecost), its fulfillment in law. The Sabbath, a willful refusal to work, was a weekly celebration of humankind's uniqueness, of people as free, moral agents; and the extension of the Sabbath rest to one's servants and beasts a sign of the universality implicit in Jewish teaching. If the Torah was not simply identical with moral law, the differences could easily be ascribed to the time or place when its specific ordinances arose, a legal system's need to compensate for human frailty or its function in assuring the survival of the community.

This once happy identification of Jewish law with ethics now seems untenable. Our pluralistic view of history makes us skeptical of the idea of an essence to Jewish law or any other historical phenomenon. Our study of classic Jewish texts rarely shows them to intend the universal humanitarianism a previous generation discovered in them. A key contemporary issue is particularism, the Jews as God's chosen people. Ethics would reject the notion of special groups, either for favor or disparagement. An ethical injunction should apply to all people equally. One reason modern ethics appealed to Jews was that no one, not even a Jew, was to be an outsider to their operation. But Jewish law knows a number of highly important distinctions between persons. Within the Jewish community, for example, the law treats women decidedly different than it does men. Most apologists will argue that this was really done for the good of the women or in recognition of their special familial situation. Others will offer a structural defense and say that all legal systems make distinctions between groups or classes, or more pragmatically, that one must accept occasional problems with the system to keep it going. These may be reasonable explanations but they all demonstrate the substantial distance between Jewish law and a system of ethics. The Torah tradition seems most reasonably thought of as a typical structure of religious practice that developed over centuries, retaining traces of what was thought proper in previous social situations. While it may be unusually expressive of what we now see are universal ethical ideals, it also conflicts with them, because among other reasons of its heavy weight of precedent and its relatively limited tradition of change.

The disparity between Jewish law and ethics is also highlighted by the difference between the duties of one Jew to another as contrasted to a Jew's duties to non-Jews. The *halachah* mandates some universally ethical responsibilities, but they are few in number and they are outweighed in significance by the matters in which Jews and Gentiles may be treated differently, e.g., until a recent decision Jewish law taught that a Jew must desecrate the Sabbath to save a Jewish life but must not do so to save the life of a Gentile. Again apologists offer historical, social and even jurisprudential justifications for such separate levels of responsibility. That only identifies the *halachah* as primarily a legal, not an ethical system, for all its uncommon ethical sensitivity. To one who is not defensive about the Jewish tradition or is not out to refute the many anti-Semitic attacks made against Jewish law, this seems so obvious that it seems peculiar to have to explain it. To those whose Judaism has been validated by the identity of Jewish law and ethics, the revisionist position I have presented will seem strange and dangerous. However, if my contention is correct, it raises several important questions. If Jewish law is not essentially ethics, what is its relation to the ethical? When Jews oppose the detailed law their people has evolved over the centuries to what seems to them the relatively contentless ethics set forth by contemporary Christian theoreticians, what is the ethical status of the Jewish law they are discussing?

Another set of problems, not unrelated to the previous ones, focuses on the modern thesis that an authentic moral will is self-legislating. Without raising all the old canards about Pharisaic legalism and the aridity of life under the Torah, one can still distinguish between following a rule because it is the rule and doing the good. Jewish law itself recognizes that merely following the rules, though God is their author, can lead to deplorable results. The rabbis of the Talmud show the moral aspect of their religiosity as they suggest ways their system can be more ethical than law alone might yield. So they have recourse to the embracing command "Do the good and just"; they commend not exercising one's full legal rights; they speak of extending oneself to follow the "law of the Pious"; or they indicate that while certain acts are legal, they are unpleasing to the sages. The status of these and other such comments is ambiguous. One cannot make it a law that one need not do what the law requires or that one must go beyond its provisions. Yet it is clear that the sages meant these injunctions to be taken most seriously. (See Lichtenstein in Fox, 1975.) The larger question, however, remains the relationship between doing the law and being ethical. While some Jews have been legalistic—the empirical factor again—excessive scrupulosity has not, by Jewish standards, hampered or crippled most Jews in their lives. How this was managed and what it means for the relation of Jewish law to ethics is worthy of exploration.

Yet it is also clear that Jewish duty is not exhausted by Jewish law. There are many things a Jew is expected to do which never became matters of law, *halachah,* but remained part of the teaching, *agadah.* Thus, for example, providing for one's children is not a stated Jewish legal duty. It is also more than a mere virtue our tradition holds up for people to embrace. If one is to speak about the ethical content of Judaism, one needs to face the complex problem of the nature of *agadic* duty and its relation to *halachic* duty. A person has a good deal of freedom in the *agadic* realm. Choosing to do an obligation commended by the *agadah* seems much more like the modern conception of the moral will (autonomy) than does carrying out the requirements of the *halachah* (heteronomy? theonomy?). Yet though a Jew is not free of duty under the *agadah* it is not clear just what it is one must do and thus just what the nature of *agadic* obligation is. When that is clarified one might then speak of the full scope of Jewish duty by clarifying the dialectic between *halachic* and *agadic* responsibility. Only then will it be possible to have some proper, authentic sense of the nature of Jewish duty. Without such further Jewish self-clarification I do not see how it is possible to give a theory of traditional Jewish obligation, or how a modern Jewish ethics might be derived from it, or how either can confidently be contrasted to Christian ethics. The potential confrontation between the two religions in the area of ethics therefore sets a substantial agenda before Jewish thinkers, even as in the various matters discussed above Jewish thinkers are likely to raise many significant questions with their Christian colleagues.

VII. Niebuhr: Christ and Culture

Reading H. Richard Niebuhr's *Christ and Culture* is a rich human experience. While almost no personal references are made in the text one has the distinct sense of being in the author's presence and finding him a most unusual man indeed. He has the liberal's inevitable tentativeness, but that does not prevent him from fulfilling his responsibility as an ethicist to give guidance or as a human being to make decisions. He knows no one can speak for the Church; yet he finds a way to describe, with great subtlety, the modes and manners of Christian teaching about culture. Amid the variety of Christian views toward society he discerns five types of positions; yet he is careful to note how mixed are the views of the major exemplars he presents to the reader. He recognizes that the broad range of data he adduces could be interpreted in other ways; yet he makes a persuasive case for his reading of Christian tradition. He knows he cannot justify bringing his investigation to any single conclusion; yet he tries to say what he believes a proper Christian relationship to culture should be. He is more than learned and logical; he is wise. To meet such people is always worthwhile; to find them in another religion, representing it and obviously shaped by it, is to gain a new depth of understanding of another faith.

Niebuhr's concern is unusually comprehensive: what does faith in the Christ suggest as a proper relationship to human culture? The latter term is taken quite broadly. "Culture is the 'artificial, secondary environment' that man superimposes on the natural. It comprises language, habits, ideas, beliefs, customs, social organization, inherited artifacts, technical processes, and values" (1956, p. 32). Christian faith often finds itself in conflict with society's values, particularly in their temporal and material realization (p. 26), in society's effort to conserve them (p. 37), and in their ever-present pluralism in any culture (p. 38). "Christ leads men away from the temporality and pluralism of culture. In its concern for the conservation of the many values of the past, culture rejects the Christ who bids men rely on grace" though Jesus himself is a child of culture and seeks men in and through it (p. 39).

The first two types of attitudes that Niebuhr examines, Christ against culture and the Christ of culture, are polar opposites. Niebuhr has no difficulty understanding how both might arise from Christian belief yet he considers both answers inadequate. More, he not only gives arguments against each but plays the one off against the other to indicate why, to him, the three centrist positions that follow have greater Christian validity despite their own difficulties.

One can find substantial New Testament basis for believing the Christ has come to teach strict separation from "the world." Niebuhr develops this theme compellingly from the first letter of John, and it is epitomized in 1 John 2.15: "Do not love the world or the things in the world. If any one loves the world, love for the Father is not in him" (p. 48 and context). Tertullian may be considered the chief patristic advocate of this view (pp. 51ff) and, in various ways, the monastics, Mennonites, Quakers and others, with Leo Tolstoy the most notable modern example, have adopted this perspective (pp. 56–57).

Wherever Jesus Christ is affirmed to be Lord it is inevitable that some Christians will seek to follow him with undivided devotion. They may hope to withdraw from the world but Niebuhr points out that as soon as they begin to act they become involved in human culture. They simply cannot derive all their rules for daily living from Christ's Lordship. Hence, they will necessarily participate in common social usages (pp. 69ff). Niebuhr raises four theological problems with this position. Is revelation so self-sufficient that it leaves no room for culture, or even reason, which operates in terms of culture? Is Christ's forgiveness so complete that Christians can found separatistic communities untouched by sinfulness and hence the common problems of this world? Can Jesus' grace yield the kinds of law that most separatist Christians have found they had to create to give structure to their lives? Is the Jesus Christ of the cosmic human drama not also the creator of nature and thus also to be found, if imperfectly, within all human creations, including culture? (pp. 76ff). For Niebuhr there is a great danger in taking a Christian stance against culture, for it can easily turn Christianity into a spiritualism that abandons the world (p. 82).

He is not much happier with the classic liberal position, what Barth termed "culture Protestantism," which argues that the Christ is the fulfiller of all the best hopes in a given culture. Niebuhr shows how this positive attitude toward civilization may be seen in the Christian Gnostics, in Abelard, in Friedrich Schleiermacher and, most particularly, in Albrecht Ritschl (pp. 86–95). The latter two, Niebuhr carefully notes, were not uncritical in their relationship to the world about them (p. 99). Advocating the Christ of culture has the advantages of giving Christ power over the real affairs of people, enabling Christians to speak to those of high culture, manifesting the universal validity of the Christ and balancing the otherworldliness that is part of traditional Christian teaching (pp. 102–108).

Niebuhr took it for granted that this liberal view was on the defensive in the period following World War II when he was writing. He therefore seems to have assumed that his readers would understand the inadequacy of identifying the Christ with the best of modern culture and does not undertake a thorough criticism of this position. He does point out that, like all mediating views, it may be criticized from both sides, in this case as being either too religious for the secularists and too worldly for the pious. Niebuhr objects to it from something of the latter position. Culture, not Christ, seems God here, a sophisticated idolatry but one that is forbidden nonetheless. This overcompensates for the threat of dualism, which emerges when one projects Christ against culture. It demonstrates the same error of extremism as does the separatistic view, only it takes the opposite side of each duality. Most critically the cultural Christ stems from too high an estimation of reason and too low an appreciation of revelation/grace. Niebuhr characterizes the acceptance of Jesus Christ, the ground of Christian existence, as "a conviction that reason cannot give to itself" (p. 111). Though modern Christians have difficulty giving Christ-hood adequate expression, they can say what the Christ in his person and his work is and that he goes far beyond moral perfection to a realm of transcendent reality that reason and thus culture cannot reach. So Niebuhr judges this view to be ultimately inadequate for it refuses to face up to the uniqueness of Christ's being part of the Trinity (p. 114).

Niebuhr is happier with the three dialectical stances, those that can bring culture under judgment in the name of Christ and yet, also in his name, find some way to affirm it. The first of these he terms Christ above culture and he sees this as a synthesizing conception. The key affirmation here is that in addition to the law given to Christians in the Christ there is a law that God, or the Christ as creator, provides to people in their very nature. This is not meant to deny human sinfulness and the need of redemption. People quickly pervert the grant of goodness that is theirs but do not do so altogether. Hence, depending upon the interpretation, value may be found in culture as in Christ. What distinguishes the synthesists is that they combine this apparent duality of concern into "a single structure of thought and conduct" (p. 122).

This perspective characterizes the writings of Clement and the manuals of behavior that circulated in the early centuries of the Church. Its greatest exponent is Thomas Aquinas. By arguing teleologically, from humanity's need to fulfill its natural end, Thomas suggested people can reach partial fulfillment, but the attainment of ultimate humanhood can come only through divine grace (pp. 131ff). Thomas describes the path of the spirit as a steady ascent but one that must traverse great chasms. One should also not forget that people, being so varied, will find many different ways to make the climb and that the faith and grace they need to complete it comes in varied forms. Living in a relatively stable social and religious situation, Thomas was able to apply this point of view to the whole of the social order. He could show how all the usual social institutions have their place in humanity's spiritual effort which is, in turn, joined by God's redeeming activity (pp. 136–137).

The intellectual beauty and religious sublimity of Thomas's all-embracing social view appeal greatly to Niebuhr but he is finally moved to term it inadequate. He considers it to be, in effect, too positive a view of culture. At its root it tends "to the absolutizing of what is relative, the reduction of the infinite to a finite form and the materialization of the dynamic." The structures of law and institution in Thomas's social situation become God's own. Niebuhr considers all such human syntheses provisional; how then can one identify them with the divine will? (p. 145). Niebuhr is also troubled because such acceptance of society produces a religion that is culturally, socially and politically conservative. To an outsider it seems that Niebuhr's Protestant activism has here asserted itself and he closes his critique with an appropriately Reformed view of the importance of facing up to humanity's radical sinfulness (p. 148).

This strong sense of the human urge to rebel against God becomes the foundation of the next dialectical position, that which distinguishes between Christ and culture yet holds them together in paradox. From this perspective one is overwhelmed by a vision of the awesomeness of God's forgiveness and Christ's atonement and therefore of the depth of human sinfulness. Grace being in God and iniquity in humankind, there is no real difference before God between philosophy, or any other form of culture, and foolishness (p. 152). This theology is saved from being against culture by its simultaneous though subordinate affirmation that God has placed human beings in culture and sustains them there. Therefore, human civilization cannot be altogether evil. Locating this implicit goodness and relating it to the basic human condition produces the well-known theological tensions that characterize this position, especially those of law and grace, of God's wrath and mercy (pp. 156–157). Niebuhr finds this sort of dialectic in Paul (pp. 160ff) and in Marcion (pp. 167ff). In Martin Luther and his followers it became a pattern of thought (p. 159).

Luther distinguishes sharply between two realms, the kingdom of God and that of the world, but he does not divide the two. Though separate they are closely related to one another. Human beings face this duality with a single soul and thus always find themselves involved in double allegiance and duty. The absolute requirements of the Gospel are balanced by God's freeing man in grace to live up to the law of Christ, at least in part. This is done by Christ affecting the self and thus the sources of human action. The external patterns and the social circumstances are not altered—culture remains what it was—but people come to them in a new way and thus may and should do things of worth (pp. 181–184).

Niebuhr believes there are major differences between Luther's dynamic view of the Christian's relation to culture and the rather mechanical, static dualism espoused by his followers (p. 179). Niebuhr esteems the existential sensitivity of Luther's teaching for its emphasis on experience rather than on rules or patterns. He notes that despite its concern with inwardness it was translated by many Christians into lives of service in the culture and it brought new vigor into Christianity itself (p. 186). However, the existential can easily become antinomian and an emphasis on humankind's sinful pride can lead to a deprecation of society's standards and accomplishments. Niebuhr highlights the irony of history by pointing out that Lutheranism, which began as a movement of radical reform, ended by changing only the Church and remained satisfied to leave other social institutions alone. Politics and economics then fall outside the purview of serious religious consideration; at best they are dikes against sin and therefore in need of religious defense against all who attack them (p. 188). Such conservatism has made this conception vulnerable to attack by modern political activists and raises the questions of whether it adequately appreciates God's work in creating people and society.

Having now again played off one theory against another, the world affirmation of Thomas against the sin consciousness of Luther, Niebuhr has set the stage for affirming the fifth type of theology, Christ, the transformer of culture, as the most reasonable Christian position. In part, this is Niebuhr's conclusion, but he also places certain limitations upon such an interpretation of his views. Positively he argues that the thinkers in whom he finds this fifth position belong to (*sic*, not "are") the "great central tradition of the church" (p. 190). But he also admits that this is more a motif found in them than a well-developed traditional theory. In fact, some writers who most clearly gave it voice, such as John, Augustine and Calvin, retreat from accepting it wholeheartedly. What disturbed them most was its implicit universalism, the belief that faith in the Christ can be found among all people and is not confined to those in the Church (pp. 216–217).

Three theological affirmations underlie the view that the Christ transforms culture. First, these believers hold that humanity lives by the power of the Word in creation and that God's creative goodness is therefore to be found in human culture. The emphasis here is Johannine, that Christ is a very present, participating redeemer. But, second, people reverse the goodness inherent in creation by perverse rebellion against God. Culture may be sin-full but it does not then require apocalyptic revision, that is, a new creation, but only radical conversion. Third, history thus becomes an open, dynamic interaction between humanity and God with the present rather than some distant future as the critical moment. Eschatology has been made immediate, at least in emphasis (pp. 191ff).

This theory is most consistently expressed in the theology of F. D. Maurice. His positive sense of what God makes possible in the present results in his considered refusal to be part of any division and negativity in the Church. He called on Christians to work humbly and positively for a universal fulfillment of God's kingdom now, while recognizing the power sin retained to nullify their efforts. Some support for the notion that this comes close to Niebuhr's own views may be found in a critique of it, which is limited to one sentence (p. 229) and to which, again unprecedentedly, a rejoinder is added.

Yet there is another chapter, modestly suggesting that this investigation remains "unconcluded and inconclusive" and could be extended indefinitely (p. 230). This sound like the customary scholarly prelude to evading an answer, but Niebuhr is too loyal to the ethicist's calling not to essay some positive statement. He does this only after taking on the full burdens of the nonorthodox position. He acknowledges that he starts from a partial, relative faith, yet insists that this does not condemn him to relativism. Though ethical deliberation leads him to no specific answer, facing real decisions requires him to transcend intellectual vacillation (pp. 233ff). He then sets a case for extending existentialism into a social dimension and bases it on three considerations: that decisions necessarily involve others, that when true they are not true for me alone but for people generally, and that while the present is critical in decision-making it never comes without a past and an effect on the future, thus radically historicizing the self (pp. 244–249). We may be free in our choice yet we exist as dependent creatures. "Our ultimate question in this existential situation of dependent freedom is not whether we will choose in accordance with reason or by faith, but whether we will choose with reasoning faithlessness or reasoning faith" (p. 251). The Christian begins with faith and this entails loyalty and trust; since faith involves truth, it also involves "loyalty to truth and to all who are loyal to the truth." So, "Faith exists only in a community of selves in the presence of a transcendent cause" (p. 253). For Christians, the cause is the Christ. "Here the great surd enters . . . What is irrational here is the creation of faith in the faithfulness of God by the crucifixion, the betrayal of Jesus Christ, who was utterly loyal to Him . . . and that in consequence of this, faith in the God of his faith should be called forth in us . . . On the basis of that faith we reason" about culture (pp. 254–255). Thus, though our faith is limited we believe in the redeeming Christ and in "the fact that the world of culture—man's achievement—exists within the world of grace—God's kingdom" (p. 256).

The issues raised by Niebuhr in this elegant study appear to pose no special logical problems as far as discussion with Jews is concerned. The Christian faith that inquires about a worthy relationship to culture seems to have quite recognizable Jewish roots. In Judaism too, God is understood to be transcendent, thus commanding and judging. God creates people and calls them into covenant. Humanity willfully refuses to obey God; its will to sin is great, alienating it from God and devaluing much of what it customarily considers its greatest accomplishments. God does not abandon humankind but is determined to bring it into harmony with the divine reality. These common beliefs, albeit interpreted in individual ways within the two faiths, would seem to set a similar problem before Jewish and Christian thinkers. Speaking from so substantial a common context of faith, there should be little difficulty comparing and contrasting the problems and solutions each faith sees.

This logical expectation, however, is partially frustrated by other Jewish teachings, especially as they were interpreted in the particular situations in which biblical and Rabbinic Judaism found themselves. As noted previously, Judaism, for all its sense of God's universal rule, had little explicit theology of the non-Jew. It had even less concern for the problem of culture in general. Except for a few isolated dicta, I cannot think of any major, direct statements by Jewish authorities before the nineteenth-century Emancipation on this issue. The difficulty is not that the revealed way, the Torah, is anticultural. To the contrary, keeping in mind Niebuhr's definition of culture as the environment people impose upon nature, one may say the Torah is intimately involved in creating culture on a rather full scale. Its teachings, however, produce a different relationship to the problem of culture than that found in Christianity. The Torah proposes to separate the consecrated Covenant community from "the nations." The culture the Torah is concerned with is that of the Jews, and here the interpenetration of religion and everyday life seems to have few if any limits. The nations are idolaters and there seems no possibility to the biblical or Rabbinic writers that they will soon give up their idolatry and its consequent indecency. So the Torah is not interested in the problem of idolatrous culture. Rather it considers it a positive threat to the survival of the tiny, odd, one-God worshiping people. Hence it seeks to erect barriers between Jew and non-Jew and their respective civilizations. The Torah, then, mandates separation from the culture of others for the sake of keeping the Covenant from being lost or compromised.

Furthermore, the special connotations we attach to the word culture seem largely to derive from the Hellenistic sense of the term and its selective adoption by early Christianity. Normative Judaism largely resisted Hellenistic influence. Though the Jews used Greek terms and borrowed certain Hellenistic modes of speech or reasoning, their standards of what constituted a proper Jewish community remained distinct from those of Hellenistic culture. The authoritative Jewish books of the first two centuries are quite different from the creations of Hellenistic Jews and certainly of non-Jews; the later accepted development of this period of Jewish law was the Talmud—of Babylonia, no less. Hellenistic culture is idolatrous to the rabbis and many of the things Westerners have come to prize most as culture—athletics, theater, epic poetry, sculpture, painting—are irredeemably associated by the rabbis with idol worship. Perhaps the rabbis were not speaking for all Jews when they uttered restrictive rules about high culture, and it is possible scholars may have been reading early Rabbinic literature with something of the ghetto's anticultural bias. Nonetheless, it seems to me that the old biblical sense of separation from the culture of the idolators dominated the Jewish attitude toward non-Jewish culture until modern times.

This sense of Jewish separateness was infinitely intensified by the treatment Jews received at the hands of the nations among whom they came to live in their dispersion. Contumely, persecution, and forced segregation completed from the outside what had been a Jewish concern from within. Which factor was more significant over the centuries in isolating the Jews from involvement with general civilization must be left to further research and speculation. The only major exceptions to fifteen hundred or so years of cultural quarantine are the Hellenistic experience of the Jews of Alexandria and the Spanish Jews' involvement in Moslem and Christian civilization. Perhaps too there were some moments in the latter days of the Italian Renaissance when Jews were sufficiently involved in general culture to be concerned about it. These periods produced many documents of cultural hybridization; almost none takes up the question in general or frames a Jewish theory concerning culture as a whole.

The Emancipation of the Jews in modern Western Europe brought a radical social change and made possible, perhaps

mandated, a new Jewish conception of culture. With desegrega-
tion from without ended, with society increasingly to be secularized and thus not centered in Christianity, with the extension, in
theory, of social rights to all people, including Jews, Jewish theories of culture came into being, if only as implicit premises of the
new, participatory understandings of Judaism. Richard Niebuhr's work, resting on many theses congenial to Judaism, raises
the intriguing possibility that his typology might usefully be applied to modern Jewish theories of culture. We thus see a new
way in which one religion might conceivably learn from another.

   Let me now sketch the bare outlines of what might conceivably be a Jewish analogue to Niebuhr's work. In this flight of
fancy I shall substitute Torah where Niebuhr used Christ, claiming for the Jewish term his condition that so rich a symbol defies
precise definition and insisting that Torah, the divine instruction, is nowhere near as mediatorial of God's presence to the
Jew as the Christ is to Christians. I believe this exercise will shed
some new light on modern Jewish thought and open possibilities of promising research. Moreover, in the hands of a competent historian, this typology might give us a useful new
perspective on the development of earlier Jewish ideas.

   Torah against culture would seem most clearly symbolized
in our times by the Hasidic sects. Their anticultural separatism
is signaled by their distinctive dress, their use of Yiddish as their
vernacular, even by the ways they walk, gesture and carry themselves. An interesting hybrid of this style is found in the Luba-
vitcher Hasidim. They allow for some interaction with the
culture to achieve a modest level of economic stability and so as
to be able to reach out to acculturated Jews and bring them back
to a proper Jewish existence. One can also find pockets of non-
Hasidic Orthodox Jews who are against accommodation to the
American culture but who seek to retain the separatistic Orthodox life-style of their forebears in Europe. There is in these several communities continual preaching about the need for self-
segregation in pursuit of the Torah's injunctions against following "the laws of the Gentiles" (*hukkat hagoy*) and other such separatistic provisions of the *halachah*; yet I know of no determined

contemporary effort to give a fresh theology of the people of Israel's need to remain separate from Gentile culture.

Somewhat comparable groups may be found in the early
centuries of the Common Era by looking at our surviving records of the Essenes, the Therepeutae and the various Dead Sea
groups. Here one can find more explicit reasons for withdrawing from general culture for the sake of Torah. One might also
see this theme, though it is balanced off against other motifs, in
musar, the pietistic-ethical writings of the Middle Ages, particularly in their emphasis on the virtue of *perishut*, social withdrawal. The medieval Jewish philosophers would be self-
contradictory were they to argue heavily against culture, but
they do see most social relations as a hindrance to a proper life
of intellect, their special emphasis in Torah. And the Jewish
mystics normally advocated a certain measure of withdrawal
from the affairs of humankind.

Niebuhr's critique of this position, that though one claims
to be withdrawing from culture one is really still substantially involved in it, seems quite applicable to its Jewish exemplars. The
irony of the Hasidic position is that it makes fully Jewish today
styles adopted from East European Gentiles some generations
or so back.

The Jewish rush to adapt to post-Emancipation equality
produced many examples of the Torah of culture. The *Haskalah*
movement of the mid-nineteenth century talked of Torah as a
Hebraic Enlightenment in which general intellect and high culture were the salient marks of a modern Jew. In the Zionism of
Theodor Herzl, democratic nationalism became the new mode
of Jewish existence. His views were so empty of Jewish content
that the cultural-Zionist school of thought was founded to rem-
edy the situation, though their secularity, in turn, kept "Torah"
limited to language, land, high culture and ethics. Were one to
define Torah in advance as necessarily religious (much as Niebuhr does the Christ), these secularizing movements would have
no place in this discussion. Yet if one does not include them,
one's insight into modern Judaism would remain superficial.

The most radical of the spiritual Torah-of-culture theoreticians was Felix Adler. He utterly identified Torah with universal ethics and high culture. As a result he gave up his Jewish ties and founded the Ethical Culture movement, leaving him with culture alone and not Torah as almost any thoughtful Jew would define it. The most easily recognizable exemplars of this position who remained within our community are the rationalists Hermann Cohen and Mordecai Kaplan. The former identifies the essence of Judaism with the ethical monotheism he developed out of neo-Kantianism. While Cohen utilizes Jewish terms and advocates the preservation of many Jewish symbols, his assimilation of Torah to his universalistic, rational sense of religion is utterly rigorous, as befits an accomplished philosopher. Much of the language Niebuhr uses to describe Albrecht Ritschl's position would seem, albeit from a somewhat different philosophical base, to be close to Cohen's (pp. 96–98). There is a special embarrassment in Cohen's stance for he thought that the Germany of his time was nationally committed to his sort of ethical idealism. As a result, he was a committed German nationalist. (On this problem see Jospe, 1971, pp. 175ff.)

Mordecai Kaplan has a philosophy derived from sociology by the canons of naturalism. The Jews are fundamentally a people, not a faith or the bearers of an ethical idea of God in history. Torah is whatever the Jewish people creates in the present or continues out of the past as having existential or folk value. With the radical alteration of its social situation since the Emancipation, the Jewish people must reconstruct itself in terms of contemporary thought. Since the same basic theory applies to the American people, Jews live among two peoples, participate in two civilizations and share two faiths. Ultimately, when America becomes a mature folk with its own democratic faith fully articulated, the Jews will no longer need their second civilization and can live fully in their Americanism alone, Torah of culture *par excellence*.

One historical bit of speculation is so deliciously daring that it cannot be repressed. Through its self- or other-imposed segregation, classical Judaism down the ages seems to have no one who identified Torah with culture. Yet in recent years scholarly arguments for the existence of a hidden theory in Maimonides have gained sufficient weight that they may allow of this possibility. For a thinker of uncommon clarity and logic, Maimonides' *Guide for the Perplexed* is a surprisingly convoluted book. Leo Strauss pointed to this, some decades back, as a classic instance of the way medievals handled heterodox or daringly innovative ideas so as to escape the persecution of their contemporaries. Since then various scholars have tried to elucidate the secret theory that, as Maimonides says in his introduction, he has hinted at in the *Guide*. One school of thought now contends that Maimonides had arrived at a thoroughly consistent Aristotelianism, a position quite inimical to what most people in his time took Jewish faith to be. He then wrote the *Guide* to show how one might understand traditional Judaism from this perspective and validate its law for the masses. Should this be true, Maimonides would seem to qualify as the great traditional exponent, though an esoteric one, of Torah of culture. Perhaps too, then, some of the charges leveled against him in the controversies following his death were correct.

One further observation must be made in this regard. Niebuhr feels that "The great majority movement in Christianity, which we may call the church of the center, has refused to take either" of the above two positions (p. 117). Yet when he says of the Christ of culture school that "Popular theology condenses the whole of Christian thought into the formula: The Fatherhood of God and the Brotherhood of Man" (p. 101), he identifies what most acculturated Jews have, until recently (see below), thought was the basic teaching of Judaism. None of the three remaining motifs can claim as great a measure of Jewish allegiance as can this one. This, at the least, points to the extraordinary accommodation of modern Jews to Western culture. Cohen and Kaplan may not unfairly be characterized as the chief ideologists of communities avidly trying to move from the margins to the center of their societies. That Judaism can apparently accommodate a greater identification with secular culture than Christianity does surely also has something to do with the more positive Jewish teaching about humankind and its capacities.

The difficulty with finding an exemplar of Torah above culture is that it requires someone whose theology has sufficient openness to culture to affirm its possible relation to Torah. Jewish theological liberals are open to culture but generally do not have a strong enough sense of revelation to make Torah its culmination. Orthodox Judaism, which has a strong position on revelation, has only slowly and quietly found a way to adapt some of culture to its understanding of Torah. Yet its first great modern thinker, utilizing the terms of mid-nineteenth century Germany, seems, in effect, to advocate Torah above culture. Samson Raphael Hirsch (1808–1888) was sufficiently doctrinaire in his Orthodoxy that he led his followers out of the government-recognized Jewish community structure, since liberal Jews were given equal rights in it. Remaining part of the *gemenide*, he believed, would compromise the issue of Jewish religious legitimacy. Yet Hirsch was university educated and flouted the conventions of traditional Jewish leadership in his time by writing in German according to the standards of the day. He operated by the slogan *"Torah im derech eretz,"* which, in its original setting (Abot 2.2), referred to the combination of Torah study with a worldly occupation. For Hirsch, however, that Mishnaic statement acquired a flavor which may perhaps be expressed as "There is no reason why a Jew who is fully observant of the Torah cannot utilize contemporary cultural patterns which do not conflict with it."* There was no question in Hirsch's mind of the superiority of Torah and the subordination of culture. There is even something of Thomas's grand synthesis in Hirsch's writing about Jewish duty and the Jew's place in the world (particularly in his volume called *Horeb*). Here as elsewhere in this play of possibilities an intriguing theme for further research emerges.

When Torah is seen as standing in paradoxical relation to culture a simultaneous negative and positive judgment is involved. Humanity's creativity has something sufficiently good about it to make the believer wish to be engaged in it, yet it is sufficiently dangerous that it must be resisted, perhaps even ne-

---

* Rosenbloom (1976) pays careful attention to the mixture of Enlightenment and Orthodoxy in which Hirsch was raised (e.g., pp. 129ff). Yet though he refers to Hirsch's positive attitude toward culture and social participation (pp. 168, 205, 341 and particularly 351ff, where the rich concept "Man-Israel" is explicated) he never gives this theme direct, full-scale treatment.

gated. Abraham Heschel would seem to come closest to having such a theological stance, for he has a dark view of the human capacity to do evil. He agrees with Reinhold Niebuhr that "the possibilities of evil grow with the possibilities of good" and adds "This is what the prophets discovered: History is a nightmare. There are more scandals, more acts of corruption, than are dreamed of in philosophy" (Heschel, 1966, pp. 142,146). But for all that Heschel associates himself with Reinhold Niebuhr's existentialist Lutheranism, he saves some bit of Jewish optimism by rejecting Niebuhr's notion of the "inevitability" of sin. "Biblical history . . . does not, however, teach the inevitable corruptibility of the ultimate in the historical process" (p. 143). More, Heschel will argue that because people are commanded to fulfill God's behests, they are capable of doing so. ". . . man is endowed with the ability to fulfill what God demands, at least to some degree" (p. 144). Note the dialectical quality of the statement. Humanity has capacity, thus culture can be worthwhile; but only "to some degree"; therefore, one must in substantial part always stand over against it in prophetic judgment. But Jews see prophecy equally as a call to action. Through *mitzvah*, commandment, and ethics, they seek to transform society insofar as it is given into human hands so to do. Here Heschel's life speaks as profoundly as do his words.

A less clear and somewhat curious instance of this stance may be discerned in the thinking of Franz Rosenzweig. His negation of culture does not derive from an emphasis on sin. Rather Rosenzweig depicts the Jews as above and therefore withdrawn from history: theologically, the people of Israel already lives in eternity. Under such circumstances the Jews have no fundamental concern with the tasks most groups consider momentous. He largely opposed Zionism, calling the efforts to use the Hebrew language for modern purposes a threat to its status as the holy tongue of a people of eternity. One may surmise, therefore, that Rosenzweig should have extended this view to culture generally, allowing Jews to be involved with it as part of taking the world seriously (one of his three fundamental realities), yet not endowing culture with the dignity that should attach only to the work of redemption. As his thought developed he moved far beyond the philosophical abstractness of *The Star of Redemption* (with its many rich cultural disquisitions) and applied his acumen to deciphering what he was taught by the details of Jewish living. This theme would be difficult to unravel in his late, shorter writings but it should also prove a rewarding one for study.

The fifth possibility, that Torah might be the transformer of culture, is inherently paradoxical. Torah is for Jews. How then can it be the instrument of transforming the culture of all peoples? One answer is eschatological. Jews live Torah and in due course the Messiah will come to create the culture humankind has hoped for but never been able to achieve. This is the traditional Jewish view. It is often repeated in modern times but more as symbolic affirmation than as a substantive commitment worthy of intellectual explication. A second answer would be to find in Torah-for-the-Jews some universal essence that, were it properly affirmed by humanity, would transform culture. So to speak, one needs a contemporary theory of the commandments of the children of Noah that yet maintains something of the Jewish validity of Torah. Two thinkers seem to have had such a view, Leo Baeck and Martin Buber.

Baeck could argue for Torah as having the power to transform culture, for he felt that its essential message was universal. But we must now dissociate him from Hermann Cohen, who had similarly argued that the heart of Torah was its concept of ethical monotheism. Baeck also asserted Jewish uniqueness in a way that can no longer be called rational religion. He contended that the universal idea had become so identified with the Jewish people that the two were now inseparable. What was originally true and therefore universal had come into history through a people and thus became particularized without being invalidated. Where Cohen's Torah remains practically the equivalent of Marburg neo-Kantianism and so can be called Torah of culture, Baeck's universal-particular idea is critically linked to Judaism which thus can come to culture with a special transforming message. Moreover, Baeck was the only major modern Jewish thinker who personally endured the horror of the Holocaust years. He apparently found nothing in this experience to change his pre-World War II vision of humanity and its moral capacity. While his major work after the Holocaust speaks of Jewish existence in conscious contrast to his earlier *Essence of Judaism*, the approach remains the same. Jewish particularity is once again justified in universal terms and validated in terms of its unique linkage with universal truth. Baeck thought Judaism could change humanity by teaching it a proper religious ethics. Consistent with this he was the one major Jewish thinker who called for a Jewish proselytizing movement.

Martin Buber is known mostly for his personalism, but he has a more fully developed social philosophy than any other modern Jewish thinker. He gave socialism and nationalism much of his energy, yet recognized that they had often been perverted. One may sum up Buber's vision in the term community, the I-thou relationship made social reality. This thought constitutes a unique contribution to humanity's present sense of its possibilities. Nearly half a century after he began to expound it, Buber's dream has put our institutions under judgment and draws forth our efforts to create social structures more adequate to our humanity.

Critics have suggested that Buber's sense of community has little to do with his Judaism but derives from his universal understanding of the two primary attitudes with which all people face reality. Is it fair to call his transforming force, the I-thou experience, Torah? It seems as much an abstraction from the concreteness of Torah as does the neo-Kantian notion of Torah as ethics. Yet some Jewish claims may be made for Buber's point of view. It sees reality as fundamentally dialogical, which is close to the Torah's view that all people live in covenant. The I-thou always involves the Eternal Thou; which recapitulates the Torah's truth that all existence, all covenanting, stems from relationship with God. (The Torah, of course, makes God more Lord and Creator than the partner of Buber's dialogue.) The Torah too has its universal chapters, so being universalistic should not disqualify one as speaking out of Jewish faith. I suggest that Buber has given us a modern statement of the covenant with the children of Noah (though he, unlike the Torah, subordinates Sinai to this experience). Within the total context of his thought, in all its rich biblical, land-oriented, Zionistic Jewishness, I believe he is entitled to have his Genesis chapters accounted part of his Torah.

The rich possibilities suggested by this Niebuhrian excursion through Jewish thought are some indication of what one religion may gain in insight from another when the two have some overlapping premises. Yet it is also fair to say that in a number of places differences between the faiths also emerge. Many of the disputed themes treated previously—sin, repentance, atonement, human nature—here return to make their influence felt in shaping the distinctive doctrines of the two faiths. Further discussion of them might illumine the comparative doctrines of culture better than is done above. Yet many of these consequences should be reasonably self-evident from the previous discussions.

The new area of division between the faiths that emerges in relation to this topic is their respective approach to finding God in nature, more specifically, in culture. Unless Christian thinkers simply identify Christ with culture, they face a major difficulty. The redemptive work of Christ, by its very uniqueness, implies the inherent limitations, perhaps the baseness, of all creation. Nothing in it was good enough or so uncorrupted as to be capable of substantially restoring it to God's favor. Only God's irruption into the creation could bring it back into harmony with the divine. With the miraculousness of redemption testifying to the qualitative gap between God's goodness and human reality, how can one now find any significant worth in the creations of the human will, the generator of our sin? If people are so perverse as to require an incomparable act of divine self-giving, salvation, how are they capable of fashioning a culture deserving of the believing Christian's serious attention?

Jewish thinkers have no such structural problem. That God gave the Torah to the Jews and made a special Covenant with them only implies that people in general have been sinful. Since Torah complements but does not abrogate the Noahide covenant, it does not imply that Gentiles require any new, qualitatively different relationship with God. They may reassert their old covenant through the traditional path of repentance and the life of commandment. Humanity is not so fallen that it must have a savior who is divine though simultaneously human. Hence humanity's creation, culture, while often perverse and iniquitous, is still inherently capable of showing the good and becoming better. From a Jewish perspective the context in which Judaism sets the problem of culture makes it much less difficult to deal with than in Christianity.

The classic Christian solution is to remember that the Christ who redeems is also the Christ who creates, that grace and nature are not two separate realms but, in various ways, related to each other. To the extent that one finds the saving Christ also in the natural order, specifically human nature, one can find a way to relate faith to life in culture. But with regard to the Christ as creator, insofar as the traditional terms are utilized, an almost complete lack of comprehension overtakes me, surely for reasons of my specific Jewish outlook. The text customarily cited for the involvement of the Christ in creation is the opening of the Gospel of John. I have little difficulty with the notion of *logos*, or of saying God creates via the *logos*. It is when the word becomes flesh, when the *logos* is incarnate and yet is the creator that I no longer have much sense of what is meant. Specifically, the problem is not in this instance that real God becomes real person, but that the person-God, Jesus Christ, the man from Nazareth who was also God, created the world or, the same thing, that the world was created through him. Some few Christians, as seen above, take the premundane existence of the Son with the Father with sufficient seriousness to seek to understand it in modern terms. Apparently the world is created through the Son who is fully the Son though then not yet flesh. The Son is enfleshed as the historical Jesus of Nazareth and then, after the resurrection, in transformed "flesh," ascends to heaven where he now rules with the Father. I do not understand the integrity of the Son through these various transformations. Specifically, I do not see how the redeemer, a quite concrete man-God, can be the creator or means of creation of the world. I can understand that creation and redemption must somehow be part of one pattern if redemption is to take place in creation. But how Sonship is also adapted to creation is what leaves me uncomprehending. This, I take it, is another example of the difficulty those who do not share Christian faith have in trying to understand what even Christians consider to be, literally, a mystery.

By contrast traditional Jews know God created the world and a free humanity. The same ordering benevolence that brought creation into being covenants with humanity as a whole and then in part. There is no problem here finding the Torah-giving-God in creation. If anything, it would be difficult to think of God in a Jewish context in a way that would ignore God's immediate, continuing, positive involvement with creation. This conception of nature and humanity, and thus of culture, seems so plain, so uncomplicated to Jews that they deem it almost self-evident. They wonder that people would prefer something far more complicated and mysterious—to Jewish eyes mythological—than their fundamental sense of reality.

Of course, when H. Richard Niebuhr gives his own position in his "concluding unscientific postscript" he does not use very much of this traditional language with regard to the Christ. Rather his argument is developed exclusively from the human situation and only later is the Christ brought in. In Niebuhr's development of a social existentialism he discusses decisions as the means of overcoming relativism (pp. 234ff), the social and historical character of decisions (pp. 243ff), and our situation of being dependent amidst our freedom (pp. 250–251). The Christ does not yet enter here. Instead an argument is made to the implications of accepting the world and one's situation in faith—*sic*, a relatively contentless, existentialist abstraction. The immediate concomitants are: loyalty, trust and community (pp. 252–253). By contrast to traditional theory no effort is made to explain how the Christ of redemption is also implicit in our situation, that is, in nature, and is its creator. This is done only after the theory has been elaborated. Most Jews could accept Niebuhr's teaching to this point for there is much common humanity and so little overt Christianity in it. Only then does Niebuhr bring in the Christ (p. 254). Perhaps the order of his statement is not to be taken systematically but is apologetically structured, that is, it is designed to bring the doubter to see the reasonableness of Christian faith. Yet it is not clear from what Niebuhr writes that the Christ plays much more than a symbolic role in this intellectual structure. Niebuhr's Christ seems essentially a Christian cultural usage. "Here the great surd enters. What is the absurd thing that comes into our moral history as existential selves . . . [I]n consequence of this [his life] faith in the God of his faith should be called forth in us" (p. 254). So "We do not trust the God of faith because we believe that certain writings are trustworthy. Yet it is our conviction that God is faithful, that He kept faith with Jesus Christ who was loyal to him and his brothers; that Christ is risen from the dead; that as the Power is faithful so Christ's faithfulness is powerful; that we can say 'Our Father' to that which has elected us to live, to die, and to inherit life beyond life. This faith has been introduced into our history, into our culture, our church, our human community, through this person and this event. Now that it has been called forth in us through him we see that it was always there . . . ." (p. 244).

If all that Niebuhr means is that the existential faith he saw as the key to worthy human existence is found by many people through the figure of Jesus of Nazareth, then he is being descriptive and his observation is beyond argument. Perhaps he is suggesting that the Christ is a good symbol for reaching such faith. This would be a claim and entitled to analysis and response. To my eyes he has not made a good case since he has emphasized the essential irrationality of his symbol. In a time when most people were Christians or inclined to be Christians it was not important to distinguish description from claim. In such a setting the former implied the latter. We live in a different time, one in which unbelief is widespread and much belief is accompanied by great questioning. Many new religions vie for our loyalty. Is there any special reason those who do not believe, or are no longer sure they believe, or are searching for belief, should utilize the Christ rather than competing symbols? Or is the Christ only the Christian way to come to what other people know in other ways?

Perhaps some of the answers to these questions are found in the definition of the Christ Niebuhr gave at the beginning of the book. While he terms the Christ essentially indefinable, he says a moralist will see in him one whose life was distinguished by the "simplicity and completeness of his direction toward

God" (p. 16). Efforts to identify him as the supreme example of love, or hope or obedience, do not give enough emphasis to his basic existential stance. "The strangeness, the heroic stature, the extremism and sublimity of this person, considered morally, is due to that unique devotion to God and to that single-hearted trust in Him which can be symbolized by no other figure of speech so well as by the one which calls him Son of God" (p.27). Such trinitarianism as is here explicated is linked to Jesus as exemplar, not to some faith concerning his nature. The Jewish difficulties with such statements of Jesus as model need not be rehearsed.

Yet even this early statement needs to be qualified by Niebuhr's consistent historicism. The reliability of the records "are not questions of primary significance. For the Jesus Christ of the New Testament is in our actual history, in history as we remember and live it, as it shapes our present faith and action" (p. 13). This sounds as if Niebuhr were making only a limited, community claim for the significance of the Christ.

In any case, the Jewish reader cannot but be struck by how little, in the final analysis, Niebuhr's Christ has to do with Niebuhr's view of what attitude a faith-filled person will take toward culture. Perhaps the one Christocentric theme that Niebuhr meant to be carried forward from his critiques of the five attitudes he had identified is the need to keep in mind the sinfulness of people. Yet were Niebuhr to stress sinfulness more he would then run into the counterbalancing issue of how then to validate faith in humanity's cultural possibilities. What seems more plausible, though here the Jewish agenda may be reasserting itself, is that Niebuhr makes modest claims for his Christ because he wishes to take a substantially positive attitude toward culture. The less he claims for a uniquely redemptive Christ the easier it will be for him to argue from the human condition to the potentialities of culture. He will also be spared the problem of finding his redemptive Christ in nature. From the Jewish point of view nothing theological would be lost (though there would be some cultural discomfort) and greater simplicity would be gained, were the Christ omitted from Neibuhr's theory altogether. One would then, out of one's existential situation, face the covenanting God in utter immediacy and allow God's direct command, judgment and forgiveness to become the axis around which one's life moves.

With all this criticism, Niebuhr's book yet raises a major challenge to contemporary Judaism: just what do Jews propose to do about the world? Some years ago that would have seemed a facetious question. Jews then were so eager to participate in American society that Torah of culture was almost certainly their predominant sense of Judaism. Perhaps it still is, but the evidence today is at least mixed, and it is not impossible that a major change has taken place in the enthusiastic acceptance by the Jews of general culture (Borowitz, 1980).

The old basic assumption of Jewish life was that the promise of the Emancipation was real even if its practice was temporarily flawed. The growth of secular anti-Semitism was largely discounted as cultural lag, the stubborn remnant of centuries of Christian sway that social reactionaries manipulated for their own ends. Full secularization and liberal social policies would gradually reduce it to impotence—and the post-World War II development of America seemed to prove this true.

Only the ideological Zionists dissented. They insisted that the Emancipation was fundamentally a fraud. Did not general society expect the Jews to give up most of their distinctive ethnic way of life? Anti-Semitism showed that a hidden, antipathetic attitude toward Jews remained a social reality. Despite surface progress, the Jews would never be accepted as equals. They could not count on really having rights until they were in their own land and thus the guarantors of their own status. Such Zionist analyses of the Emancipation convinced few Jews in the early decades of the twentieth century. Those who emigrated from the center of Jewish population in Eastern Europe went to the Western democracies, if they were able to gain entry, not to Palestine. Only with Hitler did the pattern of migration change and then because the democracies refused to admit many Jewish refugees. The British even cut off immigration to Palestine. The horror of the Holocaust under Hitler is made more tragic when one recalls that many of the Jews who were prepared to leave Germany could find no place to go. The Nazis under Hitler

killed 6 million Jews and millions of Gypsies, Communists, ho-
mosexuals and others as well, some estimates of the total going
to 16 or 18 million. These deaths cannot be considered war ca-
sualties. They were the result of a deliberate, rational, methodical effort at extermination. The Holocaust was not a sudden
burst of mass hysteria but a bureaucratically organized and developed program that ran for years. Not a few officials found
their careers and life's labors in it. It was not the rampage of a
barbaric horde but the program of a nation that led world science, culture and intellectuality, that was the cradle of Protestantism and once seemed as devout a Christian nation as the
world knew. Irving Greenberg has argued that the Holocaust
brought the Jewish Emancipation era to a close. (In 1975, pp.
534–536 he extends this view to all modernity.)

Nearly two decades passed before the American Jewish
community could bring itself to begin assessing and assimilating
the meaning of what had happened. Perhaps it was the capture
and trial of Eichmann, or the civil rights and anti-Vietnam War
struggles in the United States. Perhaps distance had made the
community safe enough to reopen the traumas of the past.
Whatever the reasons, the Holocaust finally became a major factor in American Jewish consciousness and it has taken on fresh
significance with the turbulent events of the passing years.

As the 1960's drew to a close American anti-Semitism became a factor in the community's perception of its situation in a
way that it had not been since the 1930's. The social upheaval in
American cities produced incidents of anti-Jewish behavior. Jews
felt threatened that society might alter its rules, taking away Jewish gains so that other groups might share more in the benefits
of society, but not at the expense of the established social
groups. Internationally, the State of Israel was abandoned by its
supposed allies before and during the Six-Day War of 1967 and
American Jews saw no Christian denominational leaders who,
despite some years of growth in interfaith understanding, would
speak to the peril facing the Israelis. It came only as bitter con-
firmation, then, when historical research revealed that the leaders of the Western democracies had learned during the war of
Hitler's extermination program but refused to do anything

about it. It was even more bitter to learn that when American Jewish leaders had discovered the truth they agreed to keep silence—a sin that weighs heavily on the community today.

The 1970's exacerbated this mood. Changing neighborhoods often meant the abandonment of areas of old Jewish settlement. Affirmative action at universities seemed an attack on the spectacular successes Jews had scored despite quiet discrimination. Anti-Semitism was spread in the mass media through remarks from notable public sources—Truman Capote, General Brown, Nixon on tape, Spiro Agnew, even *Time* magazine reminding its readers that Prime Minister Begin's name was pronounced like Fagin. The very liberalism that had once seemed the best way to gain rights for all groups now seemed out of effective ideas or, where it had them, as in the case of busing, they often seemed inimical to Jewish interests. The new ethnicity made group self-assertion acceptable but that brought a freshly cynical self-interest into American politics. Jews did not see other groups as so much concerned about gaining rights for all minorities as in enlarging their own piece of the pie. It was a special shock to learn that for many government programs Jews were not considered a minority.

International developments made Jews doubly defensive. The State of Israel remained threatened and insecure. With the oil cartel's new power, the Israelis were abandoned by all their major international supporters save the United States, and that country was pressuring them for an agreement with their neighbors that would conform to American needs. The most dramatic, if not the most important, area of Jewish reverses was the United Nations. No group of Americans had been as fervent in its hopes for and its support of the United Nations as were American Jews. They devoutly believed that a proper international forum would mean the rule of rationality and morality among nations. But then the United Nations welcomed the terrorist, Yasir Arafat, to its rostrum and in gathering after gathering of its associated bodies voted condemnations of the State of Israel regardless of the substance of the proposals.

Let us place Jewish fearfulness in its greater social context. In the wake of the post-Vietnam War disillusion and the Watergate era scandals—not those of the White House alone—many Americans have lost much of their previous social hope and have turned inward, to self, to home and family, to their ethnic community. An age of political protest and social experimentation has given way to a time of quiet despair and compensatory self-indulgence, of disbelief in the worth of great programs and skepticism about significant social betterment, of simple fear that muggers or chance or some other irrationality will not let us enjoy what we have. The mood may pass, as did the vaguely analogous, self-satisfied Eisenhower era. In the meantime society and self-government seem too much for most people to cope with.

The general social mood regularly gains extra power as it is reflected in the Jewish community. In a time when paranoia seems almost a part of normality, American Jewry, still hurting from its special experience in the past decade, is understandably more withdrawn and self-centered than at any time since it began to leave its immigrant isolation. The voice of general social concern is still heard among Jews but only rarely and weakly. Today social action in the Jewish community means help for other Jews, mostly in the Soviet Union and the State of Israel. Any appeal for American or world issues is likely to be scrutinized to see what service its sponsors have given to imperiled Jews. The popular Jewish social theory is negativistic in accord with its sense of realism. Its first premise is that no one will help Jews in a crisis but other Jews. Thus in the present social disintegration Jews need not justify being concerned essentially with their own. All morality begins with self-preservation; the ethics of Judaism begins with Jews. This view can be bolstered theologically by the Jewish doctrine that the Jews serve humanity by Messianic indirection, by observing the Torah and being good Jews. Classic Jewish duty is primarily directed within the community. In our world such a position seems like simple prudence. (Note the tone as well as the content of Petuchowski's chapter in Fox, 1975, pp. 102ff.) This mood of self-concern is about as close as one comes to a Jewish theory of culture today. So the universalism of Hermann Cohen and Leo Baeck now seems irrelevant. If anything Mordecai Kaplan teaches us ethnicity, Franz Rosenzweig the need for law, Abraham Heschel the inner life of commandment and Martin Buber identification with the Hebraic spirit and a somewhat impractical because spiritual Zionism. To raise the question of a Jewish theology of general culture seems, to a community obsessed with the issue of survival, intolerably unrealistic.

Yet to our society and the Jewish community H. Richard Niebuhr still comes and asks: what do you then believe and propose to do about the culture in which for all your complaints and despairing you are obviously a participant and of which you are still so greatly a beneficiary? Though you emphatically reject the Christ/Torah of culture, can you honestly affect the stance of Christ/Torah against culture? If you do not believe enough in culture or in your faith to have Christ/Torah above culture, are you ready to settle for Christ/Torah in paradox with culture, thus effectively abandoning the cultural realm to its present harmful patterns? Is there not something about Messianic faith which requires that Christ/Torah somehow work now and not just in the End of Days to transform culture? Are we human beings so helpless for all our genius at sinning that with God's help we can do nothing to move our society and perhaps our world a bit closer to the realization of the kingdom? Though we cannot do much of the righteousness we ought to do, is it a proper service of God not to do such social righteousness as we might do?

Such questions arise from Richard Niebuhr's pages with prophetic power. I have come across them in the writings of the teachers and masters of my community, but I have not been forced to face them with such intellectual precision as when Niebuhr's luminous analysis of our response to culture brought them to full self-consciousness. His Christian conscience has given new sensitivity to my Jewish sense of obligation. Apparently such a result too is part of the logic of interreligious discourse.

VIII. Christology: Does It Lead to Anti-Semitism?

Rosemary Ruether has called anti-Semitism "the left hand of Christology" (1974, p. 2), described christology as "the other side of anti-Judaism" (p. 246) and said that "Christology and anti-Judaism intertwine" (p. 226). To what extent are these judgments true of the christological theories studied here? A preliminary typological hypothesis may help sensitize us to the possibilities. Traditionalist theologians, being deeply respectful of New Testament teaching, would seem likely to carry forward the anti-Jewish tendencies found there. Liberal theologians, being deeply concerned with the bonds that unite all humanity despite cultural differences, will consider it a particular responsibility to disavow anti-Semitism and will create theologies with that in mind. Post-liberal theologians, being open to the call of tradition while they seek to give it a substantial foundation in reason, might wind up at either end of the spectrum. But in reality, to what extent might Jewish readers find what they would consider anti-Semitic themes in the theologies studied in this book?

Karl Barth treated the question of the Jews and Judaism in several places in the *Church Dogmatics*.* His doctrine of the Jews

* I am grateful to Prof. Steven S. Schwarzschild for providing me with the references in the German originals. I cite them here in the English translations: II, 2; 195–305. III, 3; 176–183, 210–227. IV, 3 second half; 876–878.

is typically dialetical. He affirms that God once chose the Jewish people and insists, with some passion and repetitiousness, that they remain God's chosen people. Indeed they are specially close to God and no Christian, because not born to covenant, can ever be as close to God. In this way Barth consciously negates the theological roots of Christian anti-Semitism, the abrogation of the people of Israel's living relationship with God after their rejection of the Christ. But, God having appeared among humankind as Jesus the Christ, Israel now is chosen "to reflect the judgment from which God has rescued man and which He wills to endure Himself in the person of Jesus of Nazareth . . . It will express the awareness of the human basis of the divine suffering and therefore the recognition of man's incapacity, unwillingness and unworthiness with regard to the divine mercy purposed in Jesus Christ" (1957, p. 206). "Over against the witness of the church it can set forth only the sheer, stark judgment of God, only the obduracy and consequent misery of man . . . This is how Israel punishes itself for its sectarian self-assertion . . . [One can see this] even in the spectral form of the Synagogue" (p. 209 and often).

The tension in Barth's view of the Jews may be summarized this way: the Church "will thus regard itself as united and bound to all Israel—in spite of the very different form of its membership in the community of God. Even more, it will reckon it as a special honour to have in its midst living witnesses to the election of all Israel in the persons of Christian Israelites" (213). Since the negative side of the Barthian evaluation of Judaism might easily be utilized for political or social exploitation, Barth makes plain what he considers the appropriate consequence of his teaching. Speaking specifically of Nazi Germany, he said in Bonn in 1946, "Anti-Semitism is the form of godlessness besides which, what is usually called atheism (as confessed say in Russia) is quite innocuous. For in anti-Semitic godlessness realities are invoked irrespective of whether those who invented and worked this business were aware of them or not. Here what is involved is conflict with Christ" (1959, p. 77).

This dialectical attitude toward the Jews is clearly illustrated in Barth's discussion of a Christian mission to the Jews. Positively there can be no mission as such for here "there can be no question of the [Christian] community proclaiming the true faith in place of a false ... What have we to teach him that he does not already know ...?" (1962, p. 877) Negatively, however, "Israel denied its election and calling ... the Synagogue became and was and still is the organization ... which hastens toward a future that is empty ... Necessarily, therefore, the Jew ... is dreadfully empty of grace and blessing" (p. 877). Yet when it comes to specifying what the Church should be doing about the Jews, Barth largely gives up direct action for indirect influence. Since the Jews have repudiated the Gospel "not just accidentally or incidentally, but in principle, *a priori*" there is "therefore no prospect of revision from the human standpoint." While one "can and should hold talks with the Jews for the purposes of information" there is "needed the direct intervention of God Himself" (p. 878). The Christian responsibility to the Jew is to "make the Synagogue jealous" by "the life of the community as a whole authentically lived before the Jews." In this task Christianity has failed. "It has debated with him, tolerated him, persecuted him, or abandoned him to persecution without protest. What is worse, it has made baptism an entrance card into the best European society ... This failure, which is often unconscious, or perhaps concealed by all kinds of justifiable or unjustifiable counter charges against the Jews, is one of the darkest chapters in the whole history of Christianity and one of the most serious of all wounds in the body of Christ" (p. 878).

On the most important level, that of action, Barth is clearly against anti-Semitism. As a matter of theory, however, is not Ruether's proposition here proved correct, that in rejecting the Christ, Jews draw upon them the negative judgment of Christians, one which is so serious that it leads on to anti-Semitism? To put it more directly, if prejudice means judging out of one's inner concerns as against confronting the external reality, Karl Barth must be called prejudiced against Jews. He does not care what, in fact, is the religious reality of life in the Synagogue or what Jewish practice might say about God's present relations with Jews. Barth's "system" itself assigns Israel a role in history. For him faith discloses reality and he will evaluate the Jewish claims to truth in terms of it. Here Ruether's association of christology with anti-Semitism holds true on a theoretical level, though fortunately Barth has insisted that no socio-political degradation of the Jews may be based on the negative side of his teaching about the Jews.

Because of G. C. Berkouwer's biblicism we might expect him to be the most explicit anti-Semite of the group studied here. In fact, however, Berkouwer seems almost devoid of anti-Jewish sentiment. Rather he systematically applies a universalizing hermeneutic to passages that speak of the Jews as opponents of the Christ or the Church. He applies them to humanity as a whole, omitting significant reference to the Jews of Jesus' time or since. See for example his discussion of the responsibility for the trial and crucifixion of Jesus (1965, pp. 138–141), the guilt of Pilate and the crowd he speaks to (pp. 158–159), and the exegesis of Romans 9 (1960, pp. 68ff). A particularly striking example of his sensitivity is his treatment of Hosea 13.9 which was employed by the Formula of Concord (the last of the five classic Lutheran credal statements) in speaking about the "wicked will of Satan and man." The verse reads, "It is thy destruction, O Israel, that thou art against me, thy helper." Berkouwer deals here only with humanity as a whole, commenting in passing that he is "leaving aside the correctness of the [Formula's] exegesis" of the verse (p. 185 and see pp. 208–209, 214 and 244). Berkouwer does not hesitate to discuss the radical differences between Judaism and Christianity (1954, pp. 141–142, 173 or 1965, pp. 11–12). At the same time, he does not wish to carry forward the anti-Semitism once so closely associated with New Testament teaching. This emerges most clearly in the one extended passage where he discusses Judaism (1960, pp. 312ff). Here I find his discussion of prophetic passages tendentious and eisegetic. I think his reading of Israel's interpretation of its election is unfair and probably prejudiced. But it is also clear that in this crucial statement he makes a shift from the Israel of the Bible to the Pharisees to what is then termed "historical Pharisaism" and thence to the general human tendencies for which these terms stand in his theology. His focus is weak and sinful humankind, not "the Jews." So while I detect remnants of prejudice against the Jews in Berkouwer, I am very much more impressed by the example he sets of what a thoughtful, humanly responsive exegete can do in interpreting Christianity from a scriptural base so as to transcend the old anti-Semitic Christian traditions.

Since Wolfhart Pannenberg seeks to speak in rational terms about the resurrection, one might expect him to be open to the possibility that post-Christian Judaism was a living faith. Instead, he writes. With "the message of the resurrection . . . the foundations of the Jewish religion collapsed. This point must be held fast even today in the discussion with Judaism. One may not be taken in by benevolent subsequent statements of liberal Jews about Jesus as a prophet or allow that the conspiracy for Jesus' death was merely a failure of the Jewish authorities. There may be some truth in such explanations. But the conflict with the law in the background of Jesus' collision with the authorities must remain apparent in all its sharpness: either Jesus had been a blasphemer or the law of the Jews—and with it Judaism itself as a religion—is done away with" (pp. 254–255). While I have seen a certain amount of writing about Pannenberg, I recall only one Christian who has objected to Pannenberg's attitude toward the Jews. Richard John Neuhaus in his introduction to Pannenberg's *Theology and the Kingdom of God* calls this passage "highly objectionable and thoroughly disappointing" (1969, p. 35). It is worse than that. To say Judaism ended two thousand years ago is to make the Jews dispensible if not satanic and therefore to reempower prejudice and persecution. To make christology again the source of anti-Semitism is to be blind to how centuries of Christian teaching prepared the way for Hitler and the Holocaust. To make this a pillar of a religion of love is contemptible. But to be a contemporary German and say such things is intolerable. So much suffering, so many deaths and the old Jew-hate reasserts itself! Such grand theorizing about history and eschatology and no sense that the thinker stands on bloody ground and may be lending the devil a hand.

Somehow, I hasten to add, Pannenberg awakened to his sinfulness. In the Foreword to his 1972 work *The Apostle's Creed in the Light of Today's Questions* he wrote, "The expert reader will notice that I have modified my views at certain points. I should like expressly to draw attention to one alteration, which goes deeper than the others. In my book *Jesus—God and Man*, I represented the rejection of Jesus by the Jewish leaders of his day as being the result of his criticism of the Law; and I went on to remark that the raising of Jesus, therefore, conversely put the Law in the wrong and to that extent meant (in principle) the end of the Jewish religion. Today I regret this conclusion, which seemed to me inescapable at the time. It involved the resupposition of a view widespread in German Protestantism, that the religion of the Law and the Jewish religion are identical. I have meanwhile learnt to distinguish between the two. I think that I can see how for the Jewish faith, too, the God of Jewish history can stand above the Law. For it is only in this way that the earthly activity of Jesus can be also understood as a Jewish phenomenon. It is obvious that this recognition makes possible great openmindedness towards dialogue between Christians and Jews, since it takes account of the broad common basis which spans the Christian-Jewish contrasts." That is quite a shift of views indeed. Unfortunately it is buried in a relatively unimportant work. In 1974 when the American Theological Society discussed this topic none of its members apparently knew of Pannenberg's change of heart. Had not Dr. Paul Meacham of the Westminster Press kindly called it to my attention I should probably not have come across it.

I have now also seen the "Afterword" which Pannenberg prepared for the reissue of his classic *Jesus—God and Man*. The original text is to be retained. However, Pannenberg's new view is reiterated in Note 11 in the "Afterword." In relation to his comments there on the judgment of Jesus he writes, "I have altered my interpretation formulated above (pp. 254f.) with regard to the significance of this reversal of meaning for the Jewish religion ... Certainly, the authority of the law ... was abolished ... but not thereby 'Judaism itself.' " There follows a full citation of the passage from the introduction to *The Apostles' Creed* given above. Thus, while Pannenberg's early work might give some credence to Ruether's thesis about the close association of christology and anti-Semitism, Pannenberg's openness to a religion with which he has basic differences and his willingness to change as his investigation made this appropriate are qualities that all good people will find worthy of celebration.

Liberal theology may be in bad odor in the contemporary post-liberal mood but it remains congenial to the Jews. Liberals, putting persons above texts, are not normally anti-Semites. Rosemary Ruether considers the issue so central she makes it a methodological principle of her christology with a resultant commitment to Christ as a paradigm of which the Jews (and others) have a full equivalent. Dorothee Soelle too feels the need to rethink christology in the light of anti-Semitism (1967, p. 109). By attending to the Jewish charges that the world is unredeemed and Christian redemption is too individualistic and interior, Soelle creates a theory of Christ as our "provisional" representative. This destroys the sort of theological self-confidence that might provide a religious basis for anti-Jewish actions (pp. 109–111).

Piet Schoonenberg can still speak in terms of the covenant with Israel as "promise" while it reaches "completion in Jesus Christ" (1971, p. 49). This leads him to such unpleasant defenses of his tradition as the following: while Israel did know care for the stranger "this thought is contradicted in the Old Testament by the enmity against the nations . . . In this sense it is not strange to find in Matthew 5.43 that the words from Leviticus 19.18: 'you shall love your neighbor,' are amplified by 'and hate your enemy' " (p. 103). I suppose I will be called legalistic if I object that Jewish texts provide no grounds for such defense of false testimony. But whatever vestiges of prejudice are shown in these two instances reach no further elaboration in the essays I have read. Rather Schoonenberg, in his curious treatment of the resurrection, notes that one virtue of viewing the resurrection "as a free interpretation of the fact that Jesus' influence somehow pervades" would be "doing justice to the Old Testament and thus also of entering into dialogue with modern Judaism" (p. 158). Assuming his good will to be real, one can then accept in the Jewish sense that the Messiah has not yet come, his interpretation of Hebrews. It argues that the Old Testament "was only a shadow of the good things to come" and "believers from this 'first testament' can be described as those who did not achieve perfection" (p. 151). Such statements do not divide us as long as they are not the basis of invidious comparisons between "old" Judaism and "new," hence true, Christianity. Obviously Jews are not the only ones not yet to have achieved perfection.

Remembering then that Schoonenberg was something of a problem case for inclusion among the liberals, we may say that our hypothesis about their likely freedom from anti-Semitism held up well.

Karl Rahner's christological studies contain no references to Jews, and the broad anthropological sweep of his thought would render the absence of such a particularist, historical matter quite understandable. Fortunately we have an exchange of letters giving his views on the topic of the Jews (1966, pp. 81–97). Most noteworthy is the tone of Rahner's response, for it is warm and feeling almost to the point of being emotional. Rahner not only approves of Vatican Council II's statement on the Jews but is sorry it took so long for Christians to say it. He is positive toward living, working with and engaging in dialogue with Jews. More, he feels this is essential if the Church is to be true to its mission. The presence of the people of Israel will, by their historicity, help keep Christianity from becoming an "ideology." He suggests that the complete secularization of the Jews would be a great loss. Rather, as a Christian, he considers it important for the Jews to continue in history as the people of Messianic hope *par excellence*. All this is said with great humility and openness. It is an extraordinary document for so abstract and intellectual a thinker. In it, christology is the enemy of anti-Semitism.

Moltmann's thought, as noted above, is highly influenced by his attention to Jewish thinkers, secular and religious. It comes as no surprise that, though he vigorously asserts the differences between the faiths and indicates what he considers the superiority of Christianity (1974, pp. 102–106, 275–276), there is no question of his showing prejudice, much less anti-Semitism. Instead there are forthright statements against it, such as "Christians are drawn into an inescapable solidarity with Israel—not only with the Israel of the Old Testament, but also with the Israel which rightfully exists alongside the church and which in consequence cannot be abolished" (p. 134). Israel, together with the crucified Jesus "reminds him [the Christian] of his best traditions, and indeed of the very basis of his existence, which lies prior to the law in election and promise . . . An openness on the part of Christians to the existential basis of Judaism automatically follows from this" (p. 135).

The christology of Rudolf Bultmann has not been studied directly here. However, in the course of James Gustafson's work on the ethical implications of belief in the Christ, substantial attention was given to Bultmann as one who stressed the Christ as humanity's justifier. Gustafson criticizes the sufficiency of such a position. "Such ethics give a critical posture, but one may ask whether an ethics built on Christ's justifying work . . . can ever provide an even tentatively prescriptive social ethics . . . In a sense this is an ethics of no-ethics; love knows what to do" (1968, p. 137). This is just the sort of a-ethical position against which Jewish polemicists have long protested. Perhaps in theory it might have led Bultmann anywhere. In fact, in a 1933 essay, which Gustafson calls "powerful," Bultmann, while affirming his opposition to a Christianity of "ordinances" or other such unambiguous understandings of God's service, wrote "The criterion for each one of us is whether, in his struggle, he is really sustained by love, i.e., by the love that not only looks to the future in which it hopes to realize its ideal, but also sees the concrete neighbor to whom we are now bound in the present by all the commonplace ties of life." This led Bultmann to a specific conclusion, "As a Christian, I must deplore the injustice that is also being done precisely to German Jews" (pp. 136–137).

The statement is an impressive one, but Gustafson made it somewhat more universal than was its original intention. For the sake of accuracy, Bultmann's remarks should be placed in proper context and given in full. Beginning a new semester, Bultmann broke with his practice of not discussing current politics (Ogden, 1960, p. 158). In response to a recent pro-Nazi student demonstration he gave three examples of where the new Germany under Hitler might be lying to itself and taking a demonic tack. The first was the Marburg council's change of certain street names. The second was the practice of denouncing people to the government. The third was "The defamation of a person who thinks differently from you . . . By defamation one does not convince his adversaries and win them to his point of view, but merely repulses the best of them. One really wins only by a struggle of the *spirit* in which he respects his adversary. As a Christian, I must deplore the injustice that is also being done precisely to German Jews by such defamation. I am well aware of the complicated character of the Jewish problem in Germany. But, 'We want to abolish lies!' [the slogan of the student demonstrators]—and so I must say in all honesty that the defamation of the Jews that took place in the very demonstration that gave rise to this beautiful sentiment was not sustained by the spirit of love. Keep the struggle for the German nation pure . . . and not marred by demonic distortions!" He concluded by saying that the "Christian faith itself is being called in question . . . and we should as scrupulously guard ourselves against falsifications of the faith by national religiosity as against a falsification of national piety by Christian trimmings. The issue is either/or!" (p. 165).

The record now having been made clearer, Bultmann's christology cannot be charged with anti-Semitism but rather with creating an ethical sensitivity that, though it carries some troublesome overtones, must be called uncommonly strong and courageous.

Based on this evidence, Ruether's assertion about the relationship between christology and anti-Semitism would have to be revised. It would now say that classic christology was closely associated with anti-Semitism, and while some remnants of it are to be found among traditionalist theologians, other traditionalists as well as liberals and post-liberals have found anti-Semitism antithetical to their understanding of the Christ. They have therefore eliminated it from their teaching. I find additional support for this thesis in Ruether's book *Faith and Fratricide*. It is a strong and thoroughgoing polemic against Christian theological anti-Semitism. It never charges any contemporary Christian thinker with such views. Rather the book deals with documents and doctrines of Christianity's classic periods and mentions modern thinkers only as interpreters of history. Ruether does not claim, for all her insistence that christology is linked with anti-Semitism, that major Christian thinkers today carry forward the pernicious doctrines of an earlier time. The possibility that this might happen is not to be ignored, but the evidence adduced here points in another direction.

IX. Conclusion:
A Personal Reflection

I complete this study feeling that the true task has barely been begun. Mostly I have been able to propose an agenda or, changing the metaphor, to map some major features of a difficult terrain. The actual work of detailed discussion or exploration remains to be carried out. I am consoled in this situation by the sage observations of my esteemed teacher Dr. Samuel Atlas, whose recent death I lament. His philosophy of human existence was based on the infinite nature of the task laid upon us and hence the necessarily incomplete results of all human striving. In this respect he called attention to the odd biblical usage with regard to farewells. The common Hebrew expression, "*Lech le-shalom*," says literally, "Go to peace," not as the English has it, "Go in peace." The latter, Dr. Atlas pointed out, has the connotation of one's somehow being already full and complete, hence as good as dead. Instead, the Bible knows, as its language indicates, that life consists not of arrival but of a worthy goal and unending human effort in response to it. Life, then, should be judged not by what one thinks one may have finished, for what we ought to do has no limit, but by whether we have conscientiously tried to do what we could do in our situation. If, then, this investigation has completed some preliminary searches that now enable us all to move forward in our common, infinite quest, I am content.

I remain very much moved by the spirit of the men and women I have been exposed to here. For all that I differ with them and have, at given points, been roused to indignation by their ideas, I know myself to have been in the presence of believers, some of the profundity of whose faith I could palpably feel and share. In their struggles to sense and articulate their Christian belief I have seen something of what I and others concerned with thinking rigorously about Judaism have been going through. In their effort to be realistic about personal and social existence while being true to what God wants and Christian belief demands of them today, I have been touched by their courage and wisdom. For me this has been a most uncommon intellectual experience because it has been so existentially moving. I deem it appropriate, therefore, to give thanks to God who has given me this privilege.

Apparently I am not the first Jew to have had such feelings. The Talmud records the following authenticated Tannaitic tradition (previously unknown from the Bible or given in the Mishnah of Rabbi Judah the Nasi): "Our rabbis taught, 'On seeing the sages of Israel one should say, "Blessed be He who has given *(halak)* a portion of His wisdom to them that fear Him." On seeing the sages of the idolaters, one should say, "Blessed be He who has given *(natan)* of His wisdom to his creatures" ' " (Ber. 58a). These blessings are *halachah*, part of Jewish law. In the law codes of the late Jewish middle ages the commentators take their legality for granted and discuss only the difference in wording between the two blessings, that is, to Israelite sages God "has given a portion of His wisdom," while to Gentile sages He has merely "given of His wisdom."

Joseph Karo (1488–1575; commentary to the *Arba Turim* 1550–1559) gives the *Sefer Mitzvot Katan* by Isaac ben Joseph of Corbeil (thirteenth century) as the source for the qualification that Gentile sages must be wise in "the wisdom of the world," apparently doing so to exclude Gentile scholars learned in Torah for whom one does not say a blessing (*Tur, Orah Hayyim*, 224). Karo then speculates about the reason for the difference in the wording of the two blessings. He suggests that the Jews are, as it were, a very portion of God. The Gentiles are distant from God, and thus only receive gifts from the one in whom they do not actually share. He cites David Abudarham (fourteenth century) as giving this reason for the different wordings, that a "portion" is like a conduit leading from a river. It can be widened or narrowed even as Israel's merits or sins bring it God's goodness or judgment. A "gift," however, is like something (a conduit?) which can be split apart or torn up; it is not that closely connected to the giver.

Joel Serkes (1561–1640), another authoritative commentator, later adds a reason to those given by Karo. God has given the Jews alone a genuine part of his wisdom for he has shared his Torah with them. Moreover, he has "also given them a large measure of the secrets of the Torah and transmitted them to the Jews secretly because of Satan." God has given the Gentile sages only "human wisdom" and they therefore may, by God's goodness, become "wise in the wisdom of the world," but he has not given them a portion of "the wisdom of his essence." The latter is "the wisdom of the Torah." Serkes concludes his comment with a Rabbinic dictum (Lam. Rab. II, 9*): "If people say to you that there is wisdom among the Gentiles, believe it. But if they say there is Torah among the Gentiles, don't believe it" (*Bayit Hadash* to *Tur, Orah Hayyim* 224).

With regard to my situation this legal process reaches a final, decisive stage in Abraham Gombiner's classic commentary to this provision as repeated in Joseph Karo's own code, the *Shulhan Aruch* (1565). Gombiner (1635–1683; the commentary written about 1665) interprets the words wise "in the wisdoms (*sic.*, plural) of the world," as follows: "But if they are wise only in their religion one does not say a blessing for them." He says no more and gives no reason for his unprecedented ruling, but we may reconstruct what led him to it. If, as Joel Serkes said, God reserves knowledge of his essence to Jews and gives only ordinary knowledge to Gentiles, then when one meets Gentile sages whose wisdom is in religion, whether Torah or their own religion, it would not be right to praise God. In the one case they cannot properly know Torah. In the other case their theology is not true wisdom since it contradicts Torah.

The historic development in blessing Gentile sages proceeds from a second-century universal to a seventeenth-century

---

* I am grateful to Prof. Jakob Petuchowski who located this reference for me.

particular outlook. At first a Jew was supposed to say a blessing
on seeing a Gentile sage; then only a Gentile wise in the world's
wisdom but not in Torah; then only a Gentile whose learning is
in areas other than Torah or his own faith. I have not been able
to find any literature on more recent, particularly post-Emancipation *halachic* rulings on this matter.

I do not share these authorities' sharp sense of the difference
between the Jews' knowledge of God and that of religious Gentiles. I am convinced that the sages' sense of truth was as much
due to their living in times of segregation and oppression as it
was to the teachings that had come down to them. So too my
sense of the truth is in part influenced by my living in a time of
relative freedom and acceptance. To be sure, I see a substantial
distance between my faith and that of the theologians I have
studied here, but I cannot say that their wisdom is only "human
wisdom." They know a good deal about the God of my people
and their knowledge has consequences for their lives in ways
which, though they are not the commanding-forgiving ones of
Torah, are recognizably directed to God's service. So having another understanding of the truth than that of some of my spiritual forebears of some centuries ago, I respectfully invoke my
Reform Jewish right to let Jewish tradition make claims on me in
ways different from those of another time and I say:

"Blessed are you, Adonai, our God, ruler of the universe,
who has given of Divine wisdom to flesh and blood."

I do not know what other Jews will feel about the propriety
of my invoking this blessing in this situation, Jewish law of the
seventeenth century having forbidden it. I venture to say that, in
a development analogous to that which in recent centuries
removed Christians from the legal category of idolaters, my act
will find some measure of quiet understanding among those
who uphold the law and its traditions.

Bibliography

Materials are cited in the text according to the year of publication and are listed here by author and by sequence of publication.

Abe, Masao   1975   "Non-being and *Mu,*" *Religious Studies,* Vol. 11, No. 2, June 1975

Baeck, Leo   1958   *Judaism and Christianity.* Philadelphia: Jewish Publication Society, 1958

                              1961   *The Essence of Judaism.* New York: Schocken, 1961

Barth, Karl   1957   *Church Dogmatics,* II/2. Edinburgh: T. and T. Clark, 1957

                              1959   *Dogmatics in Outline.* New York: Harper and Row, 1959

                              1960   *The Humanity of God.* Richmond: John Knox Press, 1960

                              1961   *Church Dogmatics,* III/3. Edinburgh: T. and T. Clark, 1961

                              1962   *Church Dogmatics,* IV/3, Second Half. Edinburgh: T. and T. Clark, 1962

Bellah, Robert N.   1970   "Christianity and Symbolic Realism," *Journal for the Scientific Study of Religion*, Vol. 9, 1970

Berkouwer, G. C.   1954   *The Person of Christ*. Grand Rapids: Eerdmans, 1954

                          1960   *Divine Election*. Grand Rapids: Eerdmans, 1960

                          1965   *The Work of Christ*. Grand Rapids: Eerdmans, 1965

Blank, Irwin   1968   "Is There a Common Judaeo-Christian Ethical Tradition?" *CCAR Journal*, June 1968

Borowitz, Eugene B.   1965   *A Layman's Introduction to Religious Existentialism*. Philadelphia: Westminster, 1965

                          1968   *A New Jewish Theology in the Making*. Philadelphia: Westminster, 1968

                          1969   (with Walter Wurzburger) *Judaism and the Interfaith Movement*. New York: Synagogue Council of America, 1969

                          1971   "The Dialectic of Jewish Particularity," *Journal of Ecumenical Studies*, Vol. 8, No. 3, Summer 1971

                          1973a   *The Mask Jews Wear*. New York: Simon and Schuster, 1973

                          1973b   "Covenant Theology—Another Look," *Worldview*, March 1973

1975   "The Chosen People Concept as it Affects Life in the Diaspora," *Journal of Ecumenical Studies*, Vol. 12, No. 4, Fall 1975

1976   "The Old Woman as Meta-Question," *Journal of the American Academy of Religion*, Vol. 44, No. 3, Sept. 1976

1978   "The Lure and Limits of Universalism," *Christian Faith in a Religiously Plural World*, Carman, John and Dawe, Donald, eds. Maryknoll, N.Y.: Orbis, 1978

1980   *Modern Theories of Judaism.* New York: Behrman House, 1980

Buber, Martin   1948   *Israel and the World.* New York: Schocken, 1948

1951   *Two Types of Faith.* New York: Macmillan, 1951

Christian, William A.   1972   *Oppositions of Religious Doctrines.* New York: Macmillan, 1972

Cohen, Hermann   1972   *Religion of Reason.* New York: Ungar, 1972

Come, Arnold   1963   *An Introduction to Barth's Dogmatics for Preachers.* Philadelphia: Westminster, 1963

Davis, Charles   1974   "The Reconvergence of Theology and Religious Studies." *Studies in Religion*, Vol. 4, No. 3, 1974/5

Eckardt, A. Roy   1974   *Your People, My People.* New York: Quadrangle, 1974

Fox, Marvin   1975   *Modern Jewish Ethics.* Colum-
                                       bus, Ohio: Ohio State Uni-
                                       versity Press, 1975

Friedlander, Albert H.   1968   *Leo Baeck. Teacher of There-
                                       sienstadt.* New York: Holt,
                                       Rinehart and Winston, 1968

Greenberg, Irving   1975   "Judaism and Christianity
                                       after the Holocaust," *Journal
                                       of Ecumenical Studies*, Vol. 12,
                                       No. 4, Fall 1975

Gustafson, James M.   1968   *Christ and the Moral Life.* New
                                       York: Harper and Row, 1968

Hamilton, William   1974   *On Taking God Out of the Dic-
                                       tionary.* New York: McGraw-
                                       Hill, 1974

Heschel, Abraham   1966   *The Insecurity of Freedom.* New
                                       York: Farrar, Straus, Giroux,
                                       1960

Jacob, Walter   1974   *Christianity Through Jewish Eyes.*
                                       Cincinnati: Hebrew Union
                                       College Press, 1974

Jay, Martin   1973   *The Dialectical Imagination.*
                                       New York: Little-Brown,
                                       1973

Jospe, Eva   1971   *Reason and Hope.* New York:
                                       Norton, 1971

Katz, Jacob   1962   *Exclusiveness and Tolerance.*
                                       New York: Schocken, 1962

Kohler, Kaufmann   1943   *Jewish Theology.* Cincinnati:
                                       Riverdale, 1943

Knox, John   1947   *On the Meaning of Christ.* New
                                       York: Scribners, 1947

Lipner, Julius   1976   "Truth Claims and Interreligious Dialogue," *Religious Studies*, Vol. 12, No. 2, June 1976

Moltmann, Jurgen   1967   *Theology of Hope.* New York: Harper and Row, 1967

    1974   *The Crucified God.* New York: Harper and Row, 1974

Moore, George Foot   1932   *Judaism*, Vol. II. Cambridge: Harvard University Press, 1932

Niebuhr, H. Richard   1956   *Christ and Culture.* New York: Harper Torchbooks, 1956

Ogden, Schubert, tr.   1960   *Existence and Faith, Shorter Writings of Rudolf Bultmann.* New York: Meridian, 1960

Pannenberg, Wolfhart   1968   *Jesus—God and Man.* Philadelphia: Westminster, 1968

    1969   *Theology and the Kingdom of God.* Philadelphia: Westminster, 1969

    1972   *The Apostles' Creed in the Light of Today's Questions.* Philadelphia: Westminster, 1972

Rahner, Karl   1961   *Theological Investigations*, Vol. I. Baltimore: Helicon, 1961

    1966   "Unbefangenheit und Anspruch," *Stimmen Der Zeit*, August 1966

    1969   "Jesus Christ, IV History of Dogma and Theology," *Sacramentum Mundi*, Vol. III. New York: Herder and Herder, 1969

Roberts, Louis   1967   *The Achievement of Karl Rahner.*
                                    New York: Herder and Herd-
                                    er, 1967

Rosenbloom, Noah H.   1976   *Tradition in an Age of Reform.*
                                    Philadelphia: Jewish Publica-
                                    tion Society, 1976

Rosenstock–Huessy,   1969   *Judaism   Despite   Christianity.*
Eugen   University, Ala.: University of
                                    Alabama Press, 1969

Ruether, Rosemary   1972a   "An Invitation to Jewish-
                                    Christian Dialogue," *The Ecu-
                                    menist*, Vol. 10, No. 2, Jan-
                                    uary–February 1972

                          1972b   "Paradoxes of Hope," *Theo-
                                    logical Studies*, Vol. 33, No. 2,
                                    June 1972

                          1974   *Faith and Fratricide.* New York:
                                    Seabury, 1974

Sandmel, Samuel   1965   *We Jews and Jesus.* New York:
                                    Oxford   University   Press,
                                    1965

Schoonenberg, Piet   1971   *The Christ.* New York: Herder
                                    and Herder, 1971

Shepherd, William C.   1974   "On the Concept of 'Being
                                    Wrong' Religiously," *Journal
                                    of the American Academy of Reli-
                                    gion*, Vol. 42, No. 1, March
                                    1974

Sherrard, Philip   1974   "The Tradition and The Tra-
                                    ditions: The Confrontation of
                                    Religious Doctrines," *Reli-
                                    gious Studies*, Vol. 10, No. 4,
                                    December 1974

Simon, Leon   1946   *Ahad Ha-am, Essays, Letters,
                                    Memoirs.* Oxford: East and
                                    West, 1946

Soelle, Dorothee	1967	*Christ The Representative*. Philadelphia: Fortress, 1967
Soloveitchik, Joseph B.	1964	"Confrontation," *Tradition*, Vol. 6, No. 2, Spring–Summer 1964
Sontag, Frederick	1975	"Freedom and God: The Meeting of East and West," *Religious Studies*, Vol. II, No. 4, December 1975
Talmage, Frank, ed.	1975	*Disputation and Dialogue*. New York: Ktav, 1975

Index